Time To Shine

Adapting who you are and what you
know to succeed in the ideas economy

MARK HODGSON

Copyright © 2017 by Mark Hodgson

All rights reserved. This book or any portion thereof may not be reproduced or used in any manner whatsoever without the express written permission of the publisher except for the use of brief quotations in a book review or scholarly journal.

First Printing: 2015

Mark Hodgson
25 The Avenue
Sydney
New South Wales 2106
Australia

mark@markhodgson.com.au
www.markhodgson.com.au

Contents

Acknowledgements 5
Introduction 6

Part 1: Building confidence 9

Finding your authentic voice 10
Are you 1 in a 100? 12
Finding your lone nut 14
All of me 15
There are no limits… only plateaus 17
Are you sitting uncomfortably? 19
Fear not! 22
Are you learning to fail? 27
Have a point, it makes it so much more interesting for the reader! 29
Time to get naked in the snow 32
What's on your TO DON'T list? 35
Are you taking the time to be brief? 38
Clear eyes, full hearts, can't lose 41
Girl power shows the way to keeping it real! 44
Your move? 46
Crisis of confidence 49
Discovering your second half hero 53
Time to jump – launching your portfolio career 57

Part 2: Kick-starting thought leadership for your business 63

10 Reasons your company should embrace thought leadership 64
Tools of our time 66
Permission to get PRODUCTIVE 68
Unleashing the entrepreneurs Inside your business 70
The C21 sales solution for a world that's stopped listening 74
How to avoid digital extermination? 77
Time to put HR at the top table 80
Time for a leadership revolution? 82

Time to get your people fully PRESENT? 85
Is your business too damn quiet? 89
3 great ways to put thought leadership to work in your business ... 92
Developing your resilience 5-pack 95
Are you scarce or abundant? 99
Unlearning the corporate vanilla 101
Old gold 102
Get more customers by offering less 106
Add some strings to your bow 108
Time to get on the radar people 111
Is your expertise ready for the big time? 113
Think twice to maximise your influence 117
Standing out in the gig economy 120
Why it's OK to play the fool on the hill 124

Part 3: Creating a winning mindset 127

Don't die wandering 128
You get What You Expect 130
You can't get ahead by following the crowd 132
What are you missing? 134
Are you inspired by the company you keep? 137
Why courage is essential in our Brave New World 140
Drive success by being yourself 145
Getting over our 'Manshit!' to make a difference 148
Bringing out the greatness in others 150
Re-thinking what winning looks like by mastering Collaboration ... 153
5 things your best people will hate 159
Finding your bravery in unexpected places 162

Part 4: Building your expert profile 165

Resilience – It's all about perspective 166
How to build a successful business around what you know (and why thought leadership is like beer!) 168
3 sweet spots 173

Nothing fails like success 175
Going global from your bedroom! 177
The power of position 180
Lessons learnt 183
The good, the not so good and the happy ending! 187
How to become an IDEAS MACHINE 192
Getting stuff done in a world of one! 194
Why we're all entrepreneurs now 196
Are you serious about your future success? 199

Part 5: Mastering communication 202

What's wrong with you? 203
Are you a Donkey or an Owl? 206
The magic of storytelling – a speech, a poem and a song 209
Welcome to Planet Sea 213
Are you talking to me? 215
Learning to listen 217
Press SEND – why productivity trumps perfection when you are creating content 220
Why selling is now everyone's business 223
Leading change starts with understanding people ... 226
Why blogging is an essential weapon in activating Brand You ... 229

Part 6: Self leadership 234

Leadership lessons from a small boat 235
The world needs you! Are you ready? 239
Time to get our brains in the game 243
Everyone's got a plan until they get punched in the face ... 248
Ready to grow? Get a mentor who's in your camp (and in your face!) 251
Are you playing in the right space? 256
Times are a changin' – and so must we 260
The future's already here – are you ready? 264
Putting ethics at the centre of leadership 268

Why curiosity is the key to our future success..........................272
My first year on the Lifeline 276
Why generosity is good for your bottom line.......................... 281
Give the gift of life 284
Why it pays to give..287
WANTED: First-rate intelligence..289
Preparing ourselves for high performance in testing times 292
It pays to walk! 299
Are you sitting uncomfortably?...302
The power of doing nothing... 305
Why connection trumps capability..308
What price success? 311
Time to get empathy into your leadership mix?.......................313

Acknowledgements

This, my first book, has been a voyage of technical learning, but much more one of personal discovery, stretch and growth. It is amazing how conditioned we become by years of corporate institutionalization. Breaking free of the old habits, crutches and comfort zones ain't easy. We need to be inspired by others already on the other side.

I'd like to thank Matt Church, Thought Leaders founder and my many fellow peers and mentors in that special community for their readiness to challenge, inspire and agitate me out of and beyond my comfort zone. In this book, I share some of the outstanding Thought Leaders proprietary IP, developed by Matt and others. I hope it helps you as it has me.

The greatest thanks must go to my beautiful family. Nicki, my wife has supported me through this outrageous period of mid-life growing pains with love, patience and belief. My (sometimes!) wonderful kids, Izzi and Felix similarly have come along for the ride, help to keep me young of heart and are great sources of material! I love you all very much.

Finally thank YOU for taking the time to dip into my thinking. Time is precious and we all need to spend it wisely. I hope you find yours well spent here.

Whatever you can do, or dream you can do, begin it. Boldness has genius, power, and magic in it. Begin it now.

— W H Murray

Introduction

TIME TO SHINE

Adapting who you are and what you
know for success in the ideas economy

TIME TO SHINE is a compilation of my weekly blog, 'Pinch of Thought', (you can sign up at www.markhodgson.com.au). Originally released in 2015, this is the second edition. Pulling this version together again offers an opportunity for reflection on how much I have needed to grow and change in response to a world that is even more uncertain.

When I began writing in 2012, I saw my journey as one of an ex-corporate leader stepping out under his own steam, determined to establish a more rewarding, stimulating and meaningful 'second half'. I've come to realize however, that the new thinking, disciplines and mindsets necessary to succeed are not confined just to the would-be independent consultant, entrepreneur or thought leader. They are exactly the same ones that business leaders, owners and managers must also master if they are to succeed in overcoming the challenges of increasing complexity, volatility and disruption. For that reason, whilst the focus here is often on the lone information expert (*'solopreneur'* or indeed 'nut'!), my hope and belief is that there's a ton of value for those working inside organizations and smaller businesses. To that end, I have added a new section on Self Leadership. I am certain that taking responsibility for and investing in our own development is imperative in setting ourselves up for success in all aspects of our lives.

The blogs reflect a period of profound personal transition – my own journey from corporate comfort to entrepreneurial self-employment (with all the good and bad that entails). Life is messy! These years have been the toughest, yet most rewarding of my life. Today I am on the other side of the trough. A very successful mentor, author and keynote speaker, I'm now reaping the rewards for taking that crazy leap of faith; daring to believe that I could make a great living doing what I love and – I hope – making a difference. Several of the blogs address this journey and how it can be best approached. For those on this path, I hope it helps.

I've resisted the temptation to revise the writing – especially the earlier blogs. My hope is that you will not only gain some stimulation from the blogs themselves, but also see how time and consistency have helped me to develop a clearer, more confident 'voice'. If you are creating your own blog or other content (and you should be) I hope this encourages you to keep on keeping on.

Finally, I'd love to hear your thoughts and feedback. Please DO drop me a line to mark@markhodgson.com.au

The secret of getting ahead is getting started.

— Mark Twain

Part 1: Building confidence

Life is not easy for any of us. But what of that? We must have perseverance and above all confidence in ourselves. We must believe that we are gifted for something and that this thing must be attained.

— Marie Curie

Finding your authentic voice

I've found that one of the toughest things to crack in building my profile as an expert, authority and all round good bloke is to find my 'voice'. What I am searching for is the real me – on paper, in video and in the flesh! It's what I think, communicated in the style I love, with all of the conviction of the person that I am. Let's call this 100% Mark. As would be thought leaders, we have to get this right and it can be really tough.

UNLEARNING OLD HABITS

One of the hardest parts of this transition is to unlearn academic and management speak if that's where you've come from. As an ex-corporate, I know how, over time, I developed a politically correct, expedient and bland language, shaped by a complex array of cultural, habitual and even legal influences. My authentic voice become vanilla and diluted. It was more important to sound educated and impressive than to communicate effectively.

GETTING VULNERABLE

In her brilliant TED talk, Brené Brown explains that to truly find our authenticity, we need to be willing to let go of who we think we SHOULD be in order to become who we actually ARE. There's a lot in this.

We must get vulnerable. For me, this means admitting the journey away from the security of corporate employment to build a life sharing what I love is a scary one. I don't know it all. I don't know how it ends. There are no guarantees. I've made many mistakes and will doubtless make many more. I am learning to not only love this, but to embrace it as part of my voice – 1. because it's true and 2. because it will help those I seek to serve far more than if I pretend I've got everything sorted.

Working this through, if you can publically portray your vulnerability in a way that is relevant and engaging, you are well on your way to finding 100% YOU. Simple!!!

VOICES I LOVE
Anyone seeking to develop their own thought leadership needs to discover their voice – even at the risk of rocking the boat. It's a big part of the equation. Here are three people I love, who have clearly cracked their voice. You just know they are comfortable in their skin and WYSIWIG!

Dr Jason Fox Love, love, love Jas. A fellow thought leaders mentor, super-smart guy and owner of one of the finest 'voices' I know.
DRJASONFOX.COM/BLOG

Torben Rick I love Torben 1. because I have more hair than him and 2. because he communicates such a richness of thought and detail with so much clarity. Very smart, yet never patronizing or 'academic'.
TORBENRICK.EU/BLOG

Chris Brogan A bit like Dr Jas but with a Boston accent. Also owner of dodgy facial hair (seems to be a theme developing!).
CHRISBROGAN.COM/BLOG

Are you 1 in a 100?

I recently heard about a great presentation by Scott Ward of Digital Infusions. He introduced the notion of a 90/9/1 rule around industry, social and business network forums such as Linked In. It means that 90% of people watch and do nothing, 9% contribute with 'likes' and comments. Just 1% of the community actually creates the articles, videos and other content around which everyone and everything revolves.

I love this observation and it rings true. Most people are just watching the game rather than playing it. That's right, 90% of your competition are not talking to the market, informing the debate or moving on the argument. They are invisible. That's a big shame, but also a great opportunity for those who 1. understand the potential and 2. dare to start.

There's a fabulous quote by Johan von Goethe.

> *Whatever you can do or dream you can, begin it. Boldness has genius, power and magic in it.*

NOT JUST A NICE TO DO!
I reckon this captures the spirit we all now need. There are now a raft of indicators (unemployment, share market, resources pricing...) that point to a decidedly less rosy outlook for Australia and many other economies. It's never been more important for you and your business to compete. To do this, you need to stand out. Creating great content and sharing it with your networks and market is one of the most powerful and cost-effective ways to do this.

PUT YOUR EXPERTISE INTO ACTION

So step up! Have your say. Start a fight! Begin to create commentary, blogs, videos, images, memes and anything else you think will help your customers.

Don't like what's going on in your sector? Write about it. Think you have some new solutions to common customer problems? Write about them? See a big problem coming that no one's talking about? Start the conversation.

This week's challenge? Become one of the 1%. Oh and the final part of the quote:

Begin it now!

Finding your lone nut

The journey to becoming seen as one of the go-to experts in your market often starts with more of a whimper than a bang. In setting out new ideas, new approaches and challenges to the received 'way it is', we are often seen as a bit wacky, a bit stupid or just plain wrong. Derek Sivers captures this brilliantly in his TED talk, (www.ted.com/talks/derek_sivers_how_to_start_a_movement). I love this. It's spot on, funny (= easy to remember & relate) and short. Just 3 minutes to convey an essential truth on how to start and build a following.

In essence, it argues that anyone wanting to start something new will at first risk the ridicule of looking like a *'lone nut'* – standing in conviction, but completely unsupported by anyone else. It's a tough place and, in reality, somewhere we may have to stand for months rather than seconds. So why would you want to do it?

I think aspiring thought leaders need to have a bit of the lone nut in them. If we want to stand out, to create new ideas and products and to attract new followers and markets, we need to experiment, to zag, to put it out there. There has never been a greater requirement for business to differentiate and innovate, or a bigger prize for those souls who are brave enough to declare their new solutions to problems and opportunities that are invisible to most – until they are not!

All of me

I was recently fortunate enough to stay in a good friend's holiday home on the borders of Dartmoor, in England's beautiful west country. Nick is an architect and in converting an old working building into a residential home, he was keen to support the Devon economy and craftsmen, and also to be environmentally sympathetic. To this end, instead of using conventional floorboards, he purchased an entire beech tree from the local forestry suppliers and had it cut into planks. As the whole tree was to be used and nothing wasted, the planks were of varying widths. Nick's design deliberately incorporated all of these different sizes into the finished building, so, rather than presenting a uniform appearance, the flooring contains an intricate embodiment of many different sizes, grains, textures and shades. The finished effect, incorporating every part of the whole tree and in effect capturing its entire history, is stunning.

This story reminded me that one of the keys to setting clients on the path to making a great living as a thought leader is to help them to unpack their expertise and experience in all of its dimensions and nuances. It sounds easy enough perhaps, but most of us develop personal bias and blind spots. We are too close to ourselves and often quick to devalue large pieces of our knowledge, experience and personal history.

We find it hard to bring useful perspective to identify what we know, what makes us unique and why others might value it! In other words, we are not good at seeing our whole tree!

I was reminded of this when working with a client named Jane. She had been struggling to make money in a technical franchise business she had bought into and was fixated on what she still didn't know about her chosen field three years on. This thinking led Jane to perceive and therefore position herself as a relative beginner and, in truth, she was probably earning what she was worth. Only by chance did I discover that she had a twenty year corporate history as a highly successful manager. Mentally, Jane had moved on from this world and consequently attributed little or no value to half a working lifetime's worth of expertise. With my fresh eyes and external perspective I could see that this was 1.) clearly a mistake from a *'positioning'* and commercial point-of-view and 2.) simply not a true representation of everything that Jane *'is'* and the value that she brings to her clients. In just a few days, we were able to work to appropriately position Jane so that her *'new'* expertise was leveraged as a multiplying extension of her old. *'Instead of'* became *'as well as'*. Her story was so much more compelling, her confidence (and of course effectiveness) sky-rocketed and her income has significantly increased in just a few months.

The most successful (and highly rewarded) are those who can be present in their entirety – those who can bring every part of their *'tree'* to bear in solving their client's problems.

There are no limits… only plateaus

I've recently returned from an amazing few days on a canal boat with some friends. At 23 metres, the good ship *'Foxterrier'* was quite a vessel and despite the kind of weather that would have sent Noah off to the shed *'just in case'*, we had a blast. There was a bit of alpha male bristling between myself and my good mate, over who steered (it's a man thing!) and we learned to our cost that you have to plan ahead to turn around a boat that's longer than 2 buses in a canal that's about as wide as one. It's a bit like missing your exit on a motorway with 50 miles to the next junction!

Two centuries ago, canals were the super-highways of their day, but they've long-since been superseded by rail and then road. They have become forgotten conduits into modern towns and cities. It was fascinating to see familiar places from a new perspective, to come at them from a completely different direction and speed and to experience them in an alternative way. It was yet another reminder of our thought leaders mantra of the power of shifting perspective to create fresh insights and understanding.

Locks are central to the workings of any canal system. In today's miniaturized-world, there is something impressive about pushing on the huge wooden arms to swing the gates on their hinges. It's a strange experience too. Until the water level on both sides of the gates is exactly equal, you can push as hard as you like and the gate stands immovable. Once equality is reached though, it swings open, almost effortlessly. It's a bit spooky! We navigated the famous Caen Hill flight of locks – 16 locks in rapid succession that together elevate the Avon canal over 50 metres. It was a great experience that not only kept the crew busy, but also provided a fantastic metaphor of the journey of developing our expertise and income. We must work hard at mastering the skills and actions necessary to establish us at each new income level, but always have one eye on what we need to do to keep moving up. When the time is right, we push on what used to be a barrier and find – like the lock gate – that we are now ready to pass through it. We begin again at a new, higher level and the process starts over again. There may not be 16 levels in our white to black belt model (thank the Lord!), but you get the point.

Are you sitting uncomfortably?

There's a lovely image in *The Simpsons* that shows how Homer's favourite couch is so well-used that it has become sculpted to fit the shape of his ample rear like a glove. Reclined in front of the TV, remote in one hand and a cold Duff beer in the other, our cartoon anti-hero is a wonderful comic observation of pretty much everything we need to avoid as aspiring thought leaders. Whether we like it or not, we are stuck in the fast lane to change and it's never going to stop!

THAT'S A BIG STATEMENT
Traditional change management strategies are typically presented as the process of transitioning a business from one state (broken) through a change intervention to a new stable state (fixed). In other words, it assumes that change is a relatively temporary state that we need to negotiate (or endure) before arriving at a new stable stage. Problem is, that's not how it is. Change is now continuous and, to become and remain successful as business people and influencers, we need to continuously adapt.

THE LUXURY OF CERTAINTY IS DEAD
As human beings, we crave security and comfort. Left alone, many of us would love to take a seat alongside Homer on the couch. Learning how to be comfortable within a state of continuous disturbance demands some shifts in our mindset and approach. Here are five that I've found that help me.

1. *Let go of perfectionism*
   It's a luxury we can't afford and one that rarely serve us. The pareto principle is a great rule of thumb. 80% good, done quickly is enough to test our ideas and products. It's about getting your

idea, project or product to a minimum viable stage – i.e. good enough to test in the market. If it's good and gains traction, you can polish, refine and perfect later.

2. ***Celebrate former achievements… then move on.***
We can tend to over-rely on and over-value past achievements and thinking. This prevents us from adopting the teachable mindset that we all need to move forward. Make no mistake, we're living through a change revolution. Business models that have been successful for decades are now being disrupted and rendered irrelevant in months. The thinking and actions that made us successful in the past are by no means guaranteed to propel us to future success. So raise a glass to your past successes… then consign them to history so you can look forward with an open mind.

3. ***Change your environment***
Prospering in uncertainty requires us to be nimble, flexible and open. We need to challenge and break habits that lock us into old patterns. Shaking up our working environment is a great way to do this. So move around, de-clutter, explore different spaces (libraries and cafes are great) and mobile technologies that will help inspire you.

4. ***Be like Madonna***
In the same vein, you may want to re-think what you wear. We can all benefit from a bit of *'material girl'* re-invention. This may be dressing more casually, more formally or actively developing a personal brand *'look'*. All have their place (I'm moving back to suits as they make me feel more confident and match with my positioning).

5. **Lighten up**
   It's a rollercoaster journey we're on. With so much ambiguity, so many unknowns, we are going to be wrong, we are going to fail and we are going to stuff up. None of us can be certain what will succeed but we ARE having a go. One of the great things about continuous change is that all of our failures will rapidly be consigned to history. So learning to laugh at ourself is a good idea (I do this a lot – encouraged by my family who are already doing it for me).

I hope some of these help. In the event you are looking for further inspiration you may want to ignore these three pearls of wisdom from our couch potato mentor, Homer.

Trying is the first step towards failure.

You don't like your job? You don't strike. You go in every day and do it really half-assed. That's the American way.

and

If something is to hard to do, then it's not worth doing.

▰ Fear not!

OK. Back from the beach. *'Fake tan man'* colouring and *'holiday hair'*. Climbing back into *'proper'* clothes a bit of a struggle and the belt appears to have shrunk a little in the last month! Refreshed, refuelled and raring to go. How about you?

I went with the family to a great little beach hamlet on the mid-New South Wales coast of Australia. It had virtually zero mobile coverage (a trait it shares, bizarrely, with a *'no-bar oasis'* half way across the Sydney Harbour Bridge!), so we were blissfully unplugged, though apparently never more than a few short metres away from impending peril. Let me explain.

Be afraid – very afraid… rather than being at an idyllic beach location, we were apparently risk-taking with the devil-may-care of a base-jumper on steroids.

The local council, doubtless keen to cover it's legal posterior in the all-too-prevalent mantras of *'elf and safety'* warned us that we daily ran the risk of:

- Drowning
- Slipping to our peril on razor-sharp rocks
- Breaking our necks
- Being sucked out to sea by killer currents
- Enduring unimaginable torment at the hands of mysterious *'marine creatures'*
- and – of course (this being Australia)
- Becoming the main course for one of the local shark population

All of this set me to thinking on the nature of fear – particularly as it shows up in our attempts to get our *'stuff'* into the market as leaders and influencers.

The only thing we have to fear is fear itself?

Franklin Roosevelt's well-worn words are a useful way into this I think. Fear most often shows up as a brake that stops us moving into the *'new'*. Whatever that looks like, it's invariably a bad thing.

According to a neat summary from *Psychology Today*, there are five types of fear:

1. **Extinction** – fear of annihilation, of ceasing to exist.
2. **Mutilation** – fear of losing any part of our precious bodily structure; the thought of having our body's boundaries invaded, or of losing the integrity of any organ, body part, or natural function (ouch!).
3. **Loss of Autonomy** – fear of being immobilized, paralyzed, restricted, enveloped, overwhelmed, entrapped, imprisoned, smothered, or controlled by circumstances. In a physical form, it's sometimes known as claustrophobia, but it also extends to social interactions and relationships.
4. **Ego-death** – fear of humiliation, shame, or any other mechanism of profound self-disapproval that threatens the loss of integrity of the Self; fear of the shattering or disintegration of one's constructed sense of lovability, capability, and worthiness.
5. **Separation** – fear of abandonment, rejection, and loss of connectedness – of becoming a non-person – not wanted, respected, or valued by anyone else.

Extinction, Mutilation and Immobilization are not likely to be major factors in stopping us writing a book, investing in a mentoring program or sticking our necks out to say what we think in a 30 minute keynote. (They are however exactly what will prevent you entering the water at my death-trap beach!)

Ego-death and Separation ARE much more likely to be in play in holding us back however. Whilst understandable, we need to be able to break free of these fears – or at least manage them.

> *Too many of us are not living our dreams because we are living our fears*

I like this quote from Les Brown. It cuts to the heart of the matter. I meet a lot of smart people in organisations and private practise who are unable to move into a new chapter of their development because they are gripped by a fear of change.

What if I fail?
What guarantees are there that this will work?
What if I/we don't make the money back?
What if others don't agree with my ideas?
What if I make a fool of myself?

The reality is that there are no guarantees. Indeed, there has never been more risk. We live in the age of ambiguity. Certainty is a luxury. Today's successful players know this and are able to adopt a mindset that acknowledges and even celebrates this new order. For example, in our teaching at Thought Leaders we plan for half of all of our projects to FAIL. Why, because

1. It is a reality – and

2. It liberates us. It equips us for success by arming us with the strategic perspective and resilience to understand that this is just the way it is. Pretending otherwise is pointless and

counter-productive (and incidentally, why so many organisations fail to innovate – as failure is perceived negatively, with blame and consequences attached).

If we want to be positioned as experts in our field (and enjoy the corresponding commercial gains), we have to be ready for opposition, even ridicule. Paul Hyne, a great mentor of mine told me that, to get on in the corporate world, I needed to have influential people saying good things about me – but that the price of that would be that there would be others saying less-good things. Our aim as influencers is not to please the room – but to inform, challenge, persuade and lead. We must be innovators and prophets and – yes – we will be wrong and fail – sometimes often. Overcoming our understandable fear of Ego death and Separation then is a big part of the mental leap we need to make to position ourselves for success.

LEVERAGE YOUR FEAR TO THE GOOD
Finally, we can get smart around this by actually using our fear as a positive prompt. I recently invested £2,500/$4,500 to work with a mentor on improving my webinar offerings. I was afraid. I thought for quite a while before making the investment and there is a natural fear that I will have wasted my money. And that WILL be the case if I don't do the work and execute on the processes that I will learn. In this sense, my fear of wasting money (and receiving a well-deserved rebuke from significant others!) and failing to secure a return on my investment will prompt me to get it done, which will of course help me to make more money through the webinar channel.

Similarly, there is no better way of making sure you finish a project than to declare it publically. I am running a new workshop on how to create thought leading content and have agreed dates and booked venues. You can be sure that the fear of failure and humiliation will ensure that I get all my material and processes ready on time.

"FEAR IS GOOD"

So we need to adapt. If *"Greed is good"* was the (awful) mantra of the noughties, perhaps *"Fear is good"* will serve us today. To succeed we need to be a little on edge, a little doubtful. We DO need to take appropriate risks because today we need to move so much faster to compete. Failure has never been a more necessary component of success. Learning to live with it, even to like it, is all part of the fun!

Are you learning to fail?

It's not often you get to use the same quote two posts running, but life can be funny. Last time out I wrote about the small plaque on President Jedd Bartlett's desk that read:

O God, thy sea is so great, and my boat is so small

It was a metaphor for the trials of leadership in complex times. This week, I was reminded of the verse in a much more literal way. You see I'm training to qualify as a driver for the Inflatable Rescue Boats (IRBs) used by surf lifesaving in Australia. My boat was indeed small (maybe 10 feet) and I got it wrong in the face of a BIG wave. The result was a spectacular capsize. More yellow submarine than orange lifeboat! My fellow trainees rushed in to help as I very sheepishly came up for air. We then did what we'd been trained to do.

1. Get the boat back to the beach (motor unsurprisingly not working as it's full of water – not good!)
2. Lift the boat onto the trailer and back to the boathouse
3. Go through the drill for disassembling, purging and re-starting a submersed motor
4. Get the boat back on the beach
5. Get yours truly get back on the (sea)horse

I learned several great lessons.

TURN UNDERSTANDING INTO KNOWING
The reason I tipped the boat was because I was too slow in making a decision. With waves, you 'go for it' or run away. Get caught in a 'fight or flight' dither as I did = free swimming lesson! Intellectually

I understood this – we'd been comprehensively taught – but I was not really aware. Now I've experienced the consequences of getting this wrong, I know. I will now be much more decisive. That's a big difference and one that we can apply to many areas. For example, it's one thing to plan a client workshop – quite another to actually run it. You can spend an age theorizing on what they will value and how you should present. But you will only really know when you run the day. That's where the real learning happens – and smart players maximize their opportunities to get into this learning *'zone'*.

TREAT FAILURE AS A POSITIVE
When I capsized the IRB, there was no jeering or blame. The whole crew got stuck in to get the boat back in the ocean only twenty minutes later. We de-briefed and agreed that it was a great learning exercise for all of us – essentially we'd normalized the worse case. Boat tips over – not a problem, follow the drills and get it back in service. We'd all gained a lot more from the practical experience than the theory and dry runs. It's not always good to fail, but if we make sure we learn from failure and grow our understanding, we are in a great place.

GIVE YOUR PEOPLE THE CHANCE TO LEARN FROM STUFF UPS
Finally, I was super-impressed by Mick, who was running the program. It would have been easy to just call it a day or to rescue me by having someone else take over. Instead, he made me drive again as soon as we got the boat back into the water. I was nervous after my mistakes, but got it right given another chance.

As a consequence, I left the beach confident (if a little damp!). It was a lovely piece of leadership – one that we can apply to both others and ourselves.

Have a point, it makes it so much more interesting for the reader!

Sadly, not my original line, but taken from one of the all time great road movies, *'Trains, Planes and Automobiles'*. Uptight adman Neal Page (Steve Martin) finally loses patience with the eternally-optimistic but over-talkative shower ring salesman, Del Griffith (John Candy) and launches into a tirade on his rambling anecdotes (and personal hygiene)

Like many great comic observations, there's more than a hint of truth in this sentiment. At its core, thought leadership is all about establishing yourself as a trusted authority – someone who's view is respected and valued. Everything else stems from this *'positioning'*. Moreover, how much you can charge for or commercially leverage what you know depends entirely on how well positioned you are. Getting your points or concepts into the world in a persuasive way is a great way to go about building your thought leadership credentials.

Answering these FOUR GREAT QUESTIONS is an excellent way to start.

WHAT'S REALLY GOING ON?
This is all about setting the BIG PICTURE. Most of your customers and clients will be stuck in the detail of their *'business as usual'* – chasing weekly targets, share prices, managing budgets, dealing with staff …. As a thought leader you need to pull their heads up to see the larger trends – locally and globally – that are impacting their world in a big way (even if they can't yet see it).

WHAT DO I THINK ABOUT THAT?
Here's where you make your POINT. If the big picture is about accelerating change, or technological opportunity, or disruptive emerging business models, you need to voice a clear view on what you think will happen. Don't be afraid to hold views contrary to the crowd wisdom. Be prepared to shake it up and throw some rocks (in fact, it's encouraged!)

HOW DO I KNOW?
You've got to back up your assertions with compelling detail. You'll not only reinforce the authority of your own view, but, by referencing other respected leading edge thinkers, again reinforce your own positioning as a trusted expert. Your detail sources should span both the logical (e.g. data, charts) and emotional (e.g. stories) to enhance understanding and deepen connection with your audience.

WHAT SHOULD YOU DO?
Home run time. Tell your customer/client/audience WHAT THEY NEED TO DO. In a world of uber-change and overwhelming choice, we value the experts who (having weighed all the options) we trust to tell us what to do. It removes from us the weight of uncertainty and the effort of endlessly considering alternatives. This is the power of PRESCRIPTION.

So I encourage you to give this approach a try. It's a simple way to start to harness your thoughts in a structured and impactful way and is also foundational to the next step, which is to turn your ideas into intellectual property or IP.

And a final thought on our shower salesman, Del. Well his response to the assault is equally brilliant (and not a little moving!).

Yeah, you're right, I talk too much. I also listen too much. I could be a cold-hearted cynic like you... but I don't like to hurt people's feelings. Well, you think what you want about me; I'm not changing. I like me. My wife likes me. My customers like me. 'Cause I'm the real article. What you see is what you get.

Time to get naked in the snow

Travel broadens the mind in unexpected ways…

So there I was. Stark naked. We'd met only a few moments ago, but lying next to me was a married woman – also wearing nothing but a smile. Interesting times! And we weren't alone. Beside her a very hairy man reclined like a Roman emperor – he too wore not a stitch. It was getting very hot indeed…

No, Pinch hasn't gone all *'50 Shades of Grey'*. I've been on the road. The scene comes from a recent experience in the sauna of an Austrian hotel. I'd been skiing – well in truth drink/skiing – with some very dear friends from my days working in Hungary. We try and get together every year to catch up on the turning circles of our lives. For the *'Aprés ski'*, we went to the *'wellness centre'*. Now Austrians take this stuff seriously. There are rules and etiquette's. The rule here was you had to be naked! No ifs or buts!

That's it. In you go. Kit off. Proceed to mingle with complete strangers in the altogether. Immediately I was forced to re-evaluate a raft of learnt and cultural behaviours. I've been brought up with the English attitude to nudity, which is – essentially – Victorian! Whilst we've consigned changing carriages to history, the average Pom is still adept at the 'towel wrap' to ensure that no 'reproductive flesh' sees the light of day. In just a few Austrian minutes then, long-held preconceptions about sex, nudity, body shape, humanity and humour were challenged and replaced. It was a weird and enlightening experience.

SHIFTING CONTEXT IS GOOD
So (finally!) here's my point! What happened in the sauna was

that my context was shifted. In the UK and Australia, the context around nudity is reserved, immature, even legalistic. If I'd walked naked into a public sauna in Sydney or London, I'd have been arrested. It was amazing how after a few minutes of *'enforced nudity'*, it became normalised and relaxed. I was able to think about nudity in an entirely new and better way. It was not about smut or sex, but about liberation and wellness. It was fun to hang out with nothing on!

When we take our thinking to market, it's great to intentionally create contextual shifts like this. Thinking through the status quo in your field results in 1.1 – 1.2 – 1.3 thinking. It's the process of (and I hate this term) *'continuous improvement'*. As influencers, we need to be also thinking about the bigger context, the bigger picture. We must ask (and answer) the question, *"What's really going on?"* This gets us to 1.0 – 2.0 – 3.0 outcomes.

INCREMENTAL THINKING DOESN'T CUT IT IN THE EXPONENTIAL AGE
Many market leaders have got this wrong. They are masters of continuous improvement. Kodak kept making better film and film cameras. It didn't shift the context to think how new electronic technologies could be harnessed to better serve it's customers. New competitors did. Kodak died. Nokia (smartphones), IBM (mobile/laptops), Blockbuster (video on demand), Qantas (responsiveness), most bricks and mortar retailers (e-commerce) are all suffering from a similar refusal or inability to think through the contextual changes in their markets. They were all there to see – IF you asked the right questions.

We live in an age of exponential change – yet most businesses still think in a linear fashion. Their plan to move into the future is to extend their past. In other words, *"last year, plus a bit"*. The gap between linear thinking and exponential change is full of both risk and opportunity. Our job is to harness the opportunity by thinking at higher level and then executing on the new possibilities.

We have to continually adjust for the reality that everything is changing. By always seeking to look at the bigger picture through a bigger context, we can equip ourselves – and our customers to succeed.

What's on your TO DON'T list?

Whether you are a running a business, leading a team or growing your own expert practise, the likelihood is that your world is wrapped up in TO DO lists. There are lots of ways to approach them of course, but one thing they have in common is that they have a tendency to grow… and grow… and grow. It's not hard to become overwhelmed with the ironical result that our TO DO lists end up condemning us to inactivity.

So this week I thought we'd have some fun with 5 things NOT to do to progress. I call this my TO DON'T list.

DON'T

1. ***Procrastinate on perfectionism***
    Nothing kills productivity more quickly than our (self-imposed) need to be brilliant straight out of the blocks. Great thinker and author Malcolm Gladwell says, *"I deal with writer's block by first lowering my expectations. The trouble starts when you sit down to write and imagine that you will achieve something magnificent—and when you don't, panic sets in".*

    We need to launch first and refine second – once we've received real-market feedback that what we are doing has value.

2. ***Forget to think laterally***
    Futurist William Gibson wrote, *"the future is already here – it's just unevenly distributed".*

    Chances are there are major advances already *'out there'* that can be applied to our own business sector or area of expertise.

If we can identify and adapt them, we can accelerate our own success. We just need to remember to get out of our own little world and look!

3. *Over-rely on the good opinion of others*

   Too often we over-filter our ideas before we launch them. We seek the security of positive feedback as a way of reducing the chances of our ideas failing. It's a natural self-protection mechanism but one we should be wary of. If we aspire to be influencers and to make a difference, we need to be bold. Boldness does not come from listening to groupthink or consensus. We need to select very carefully those we listen to.

4. *Fear Failure*

   I recently had a conversation with a very successful international exec about the differences in doing business in different markets. We agreed that it's easier to do business in Australia than the UK and he said the US was better again – in large part because of the different attitude to risk and failure. At Thought Leaders, we specifically plan that half of our projects will fail! We do so because 1. It's a business reality and 2. It removes the stigma and negative mindsets (and attendant blockages (e.g. point1). Somewhat perversely, adopting a positive attitude to failure is a big step towards achieving success.

5. *Die Wondering*

   Unless you think you are *'coming back'* as a cat, an Egyptian pharaoh or Barack Obama, you'll get one chance at making a difference (whatever that means for you). In my world, I've recently learned of several friends who have been impacted by serious illness – each one a reminder that nothing is forever. If we are going to spend 40, 50, 60 hours a week working (and most of my corporate clients are in the 50-60 bracket), doesn't it make sense for us to strive to produce something we can be proud of? Shouldn't we all be aiming to mimic the inimitable Mr Jobs in attempting to put our own 'dent in the universe'.

Are you taking the time to be brief?

Not so very long ago, futurists were telling us that we'd all need to find new ways to fill the hours of extra leisure time created by labour-saving technologies. Like flying cars, robot maids and jet packs, these starry-eyed predictions now seem laughably wide of the mark. In fact, study after study tells us that we've never been busier.

In less than a decade we've gone from not knowing enough to being immersed in a *'data deluge'* of information. As Mitch Kapor (inventor of the Lotus computer language) famously puts it,

> *Getting information off the Internet is like taking a drink from a fire hydrant.*

We are overwhelmed and simply lack the time and mental bandwidth to decipher what we want and need. Communicating has never been more challenging.

SAY LESS TO SAY MORE

So none of us has any time (except my cats, who seem to luxuriate in a parallel universe!). This has created a new business imperative. We need to communicate with ruthless efficiency. We need to be short (but not lose meaning). We need to smarten it down. I call this the art of *'simplexity'* and – like most simple things – it's hard to achieve.

In a suitably pithy white paper (no one has time to read a 20,000 word bore-fest – however worthy), communications expert Joe McCormack lists the *7 sins of Brevity*. In the spirit of the topic, I've shortened this to 5!

MCCORMACK'S 5 'SINS OF BREVITY'

1. *Cowardice.* We hide behind meaningless words and don't have the guts to be clear and take a stand. We wrap our message with mounds of jargon and business buzzwords.

2. *Self-absorbed.* We are disrespectful of other people's time. When they talk to us, we're impatient, but when we have the floor, time seems to stand still.

3. *Comfort breeds sloppiness.* We get loose with words with our closest collaborators. Familiarity leads to contempt—and lack of brevity. Our double standard means we're succinct with important people, yet long-winded with partners.

4. *Confusion.* We choose to think out loud when it is still not clear to you what we're thinking. When ideas start germinating, they'll likely be illogical and out of order, indistinct and blurry.

5. *Complication.* We firmly believe that there are some things that are too complicated to be simplified—even though the world values simplicity. We opt to over explain than to boil down an idea.

As you can see, Joe's a pretty direct guy. Whilst I'd soften the language a tad, his points are well-made and I know I wrestle with a few of them myself. Here are just a few reasons why.

1. We've been educated that more is better (think exam word counts, long meetings, 45 minute speaking slots).
2. We often measure inputs rather than outputs.
3. We default to selling time, not value.

THE FIRST STEP IS IN OUR HEAD

The high-performance leaders and entrepreneurs I know, *'get'* the principles of brevity and use them to get more done more quickly and leverage the value of their output. Mastering brevity starts with shifting our mindset. We've just got to get over our own well-worn personal and corporate habits. Once we've done this, learning the techniques of brevity is relatively easy (though we do need to make sure we explain the new approach to our world as it can be misconstrued as rudeness).

BE BRILLIANT, EFFECTIVE AND HOME FOR SUPPER!

So have a go. Be brief. Cut the puff. Ruthlessly edit to get to the essence of what you have to say. It might just be the key to creating commercial success AND that much-promised (but seldom seen) free time.

Clear eyes, full hearts, can't lose

THE GAME THEY PLAY IN HEAVEN
In 2014, my son and I, with an intimate group of 140 other dads and boys, went on an Under-14s rugby tour to Fiji. It was the culmination of many shared years, some of the boys having played together since they were 7. It was a fantastic rugby tour, but it wasn't really about the rugby. We visited orphanages, painted a local school and grew in our awareness of how privileged our lives are. It was about a group of young men sharing an experience and becoming all the richer for it. It was about being a part of something bigger than just us.

"CLEAR EYES. FULL HEARTS. CAN'T LOSE."
This mantra comes from the brilliant TV series, *'Friday Night Lights'*. It's set against the backdrop of high school football in Dillon, a small town in Texas. In this community, the football and the team's success is everything. The entire town turns out each Friday night to support their local heroes. Everyone from the gas pump attendant to the waitress at the diner has an opinion and the pressure on the teenage players to win is intense. So the series is about an American football team playing football. Except it's not. In fact it's not about sport at all. It's about adolescence, adversity, relationships and families. It's about shared experience, change and what it takes to overcome fears to become a better person. In many ways it's just a larger version of our own Fiji experience.

WWCTD? (*WHAT WOULD COACH TAYLOR DO?*)
The lines are Coach Eric Taylor's. He's the mentor we'd all love in our lives; hard, uncompromising, driven, yet wise, compassionate and fair. Before each game, they are the last words he says to

the players as they leave the locker room to enter the field of play – gladiators primed for the contest. It's their team chant. The six words represent his entire philosophy, crystallised.

'Clear eyes' – Stay above emotion and find a way to get to your goal.
'Full hearts' – Be brave – even when you are afraid. Know you have given your all.
'Can't lose' – If you do this, you will win every time – even if you lose on the scoreboard.

(Imagine this, starting quietly with one voice and then repeated – building to a crescendo, shouted out by an amped-up squad of young men about to test their mettle).

"Clear eyes, full hearts, can't lose
Clear Eyes, Full Hearts, Can't Lose
CLEAR EYES, FULL HEARTS, CAN'T LOSE"

I LOVE this. More than that, I think we can use it. We can learn as much from these words as the fictional Dillon Panthers. You see, I believe these sentiments are exactly what we need to succeed in carving our own success as leaders, change-makers and influencers.

CLEAR EYES
We've got to see the bigger picture. We've got to understand what's really going on and connect it to those we lead or seek to help. We can't afford to be distracted by popular, lazy thinking or worried about the good opinion of others. We must be urgent and inspirational.

FULL HEARTS
We must be courageous, which literally means *'to be full of heart'*. We must stand for what we believe. We must unshackle ourselves

from our inner fears. We ARE good enough. We have something of value. We must not die wondering!

CAN'T LOSE

We all know so many people who fail this test – afraid to step up and step out. I respect anyone who has the bravery to take action and to test themselves and their ideas in their business or the marketplace. Yes, it's a hard road. At times it can appear bleak and we will feel vulnerable. But the rewards are great. Even before we start to make the money that will surely come, we have already won!

Girl power shows the way to keeping it real!

There's been a lot of talk recently in Australia about feminism and female role models. Foreign Minister, Julie Bishop is killing it on the world and home stage – capable, persuasive and elegant. The rest of the Abbot cabinet are about as popular as a bar of soap at a teenage boys' sleepover party, but Julie is winning hearts and minds across the planet.

At the same time, Gail Kelly, has just announced her retirement as CEO of Westpac Bank. She's been phenomenally successful, put people and culture at the core of her leadership and (according to an 'inside source' I know who shares a low-key local pizza joint with her) is also a down-to-earth and approachable human being. $13 million a year in salary and benefits is enough to turn many people's heads, but not our Gail's it seems. So why are so many women so good at getting great stuff done in what many still feel is a man-centric world?

I MAY KNOW WHY

I recently shared a seminar with a fellow Thought Leaders partner, Christina Guidotti. We ran a great session on thought leadership for HR Leaders – all of whom were women. I was the token male and I was amazed at how quickly Christina got down to meaningful conversation with our guests. Within just a few minutes we'd cut through the initial awkwardness and formality that hangs around any new meeting. We were talking about real issues, real problems, real needs and real solutions.

MEN HAVE A LOT TO LEARN

Men are crap at this. A recent article in the *'Weekend Australian',*

'Why men do it tougher in the golden years', discussed several research pieces – each supporting the view that men are pretty poor at communicating at a meaningful level. We have professional networks and contacts – some of whom we have known for years. Problem is this *'knowing'* is at such a superficial level that often very little personal, 'real' and ultimately meaningful information is shared. A lot of us find it difficult to display our vulnerability. We see it as a form of weakness as Dr Brenè Brown exposes so powerfully in her TED talk, *'The Power of Vulnerability'*. The irony is that it's only when we get comfortable with sharing our vulnerability that we are truly empowered.

TIME TO GET IN TOUCH WITH OUR SOFTER SIDE BOYS!
I learned so much from working with Christina and our HR partners. I realised that I've been wasting so much time and energy in platitudes, formalities and posturing (learnt over 25 years of corporate career-building). From now on I am all about cutting to the chase. What's really going on in your world? How are you feeling? How can I help?

Your move?

My wife, Nicki and I went through a decade of moving home pretty much every year. From North to South London. From the UK to Hungary and four more times within Budapest. Across the world to Sydney. Bondi (almost a legal requirement for incoming *'Poms'*), Eastern Suburbs, Northern Beaches (twice). Finally we were done! Nine times in as many years, we went through the pain of packing. Occasionally we paid people to pack for us. It seems like a great idea, but never really works. You see, packers unthinkingly pack **everything**. It's convenient, but not effective. To move forward, to ensure we are not just dragging a ton of irrelevant baggage around the planet, we need to make decisions. Hundreds of them – and they are exhausting. 'BEDROOM 1', 'KITCHEN', 'STORAGE', 'TIP', 'DELICATE', 'VALUABLES' – on and on it goes.

THE TRICK IS TO LEAVE THE RIGHT STUFF BEHIND
The art of a great move is to use the opportunity to prune our lives for future growth. What do we need going forward? What's no longer serving us? What is it time to throw out? When we do this well, we are not just in a new place physically – we've also built a foundation for our personal and professional success.

EVERYTHING STARTS WITH DECISION
There's no better time to *'clean house'* than at the end of the year. The good news of course is that you don't have to go through the physical drama of moving (remember, the third most stressful life event after death and divorce!) to reap the benefits. You DO need to make choices and then put energy into making them happen. As my model below shows, there are four places we can find ourselves – *Frozen, Frenzied, Frustrated* and *Focused*. Only one of them is a good place to live!

FROZEN (*ALL AHEAD SLOW*)

If you feel stuck, don't really know what you want and have low energy, you are '*Frozen*'. This manifests as doing the same thing over and over with no sense of progression. To move forward, you need to make some decisions, which literally means to 'cut off choice'. It may be useful to ask someone you respect for advice. You'll also need to create momentum. One good way to do this is to impose a deadline on yourself. E.g. *"I am not leaving my desk on Friday until I have set 3 clear goals and an implementation plan for the next 90 days"*. It sounds daft, but it can work for those stuck in a world full of possibilities but without either direction or motion.

FRENZIED (*SPINNING YOUR WHEELS*)

If you are running around like a headless chicken, never have any time, but are not clear on what you are achieving, chances are you live in the world of '*Frenzied*'. I see a lot of frenzied people. They have a lack of clarity and frequently use their 'busyness' as an excuse to avoid change. As a recent meme noted, *"I'm too busy" is the grown up version of the dog ate my homework!*

To move from *frenzied* to *focused*, we need to measure **outcomes**, not inputs. What are the things you do that take a lot of time and effort, yet deliver little benefit? In his excellent productivity book, '*The 4-Hour work Week*', Tim Ferris used this idea, (especially around the Pareto Principle – or 80:20 rule) to measure and then concentrate his efforts ONLY on the things that maximised outputs. He calculated that 20% of his customers accounted for 80% of his profit. So he sacked the unproductive customers and saved a mountain of time which he then spent finding more customers exactly like his best ones.

If you feel frenzied, some good cures are to measure the outputs of your efforts, work out what to stop doing (e.g. stop travelling to meetings and run them virtually instead) and to get clear on what you are trying to achieve. In other words, you need to make some decisions!

FRUSTRATED (*CAN I HAVE A PUSH?*)
You have decided what you want to do, who you want to work with and how you will succeed commercially. That's 3 BIG TICKS, but getting started can be tricky. It's easy to become *Frustrated*. This should only be a temporary phase, but can become permanent. Many of the people we work with through the *Thought Leaders* community start in this space.

You need to get yourself out there and known. You may want to give free seminars of webinars to your market. You'll definitely need to build a network (LinkedIn is a good tool) and you should be writing a regular business blog. Investing in a great mentor is also essential.

FOCUSED (*WARP SPEED SCOTTIE*)
This of course is where you want to be. You are crystal clear on what you want and how that will create the commercial returns you need. You are highly active, yet productive. You are '*Focused*' – which is the foundation for your ongoing success.

START TODAY
As we look forward to a new year, it's a great opportunity to think about where we want to be. You probably won't be moving home, but you should definitely be thinking about moving on. That way you'll be in the best position to succeed.

Crisis of confidence

I am a big rugby union fan. At the weekend, England took on the un-fancied Italians in their annual 6 Nations competition fixture. The 'Azzuri' excel in coffee, cuisine and love, but the expectation was for an easy win for the competition leaders. Whilst they ultimately prevailed, it wasn't without drama. The Italians exploited rule technicalities that enabled their players to position themselves in unexpected places. The English were clearly confused. Their advantage in power, player quality and financial resources (England being by far the wealthiest rugby union) was neutralised. The clever Italian tactics forced them back time and again. They were playing in the wrong space.

THE GAME HAS CHANGED

As leaders, we need to make sure we are not similarly distracted. I believe too many businesses allow their leaders to focus on the wrong things. They get pulled into (or find comfort in) day-to-day detail and become lost in management. In our fast-changing business world, that's a recipe for disaster. Successful leaders must be focused on the bigger-picture, obsessed with answering two questions. Where are going? How will we get there? My model below explains:

ARE YOU PLAYING IN THE RIGHT SPACE?

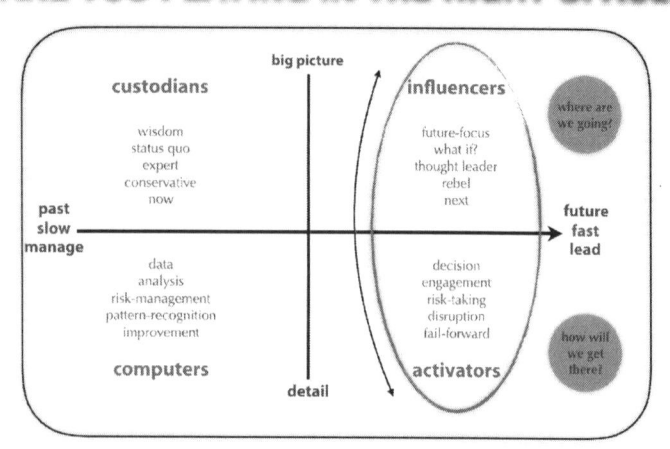

```
                          big picture
         custodians          |        influencers
                             |                           where are
           wisdom            |       future-focus        we going?
           status quo        |       what if?
           expert            |       thought leader
           conservative      |       rebel
past       now               |       next                future
slow ────────────────────────┼──────────────────────►    fast
manage                       |                           lead
           data              |       decision
           analysis          |       engagement
           risk-management   |       risk-taking
           pattern-recognition|      disruption          how will
           improvement       |       fail-forward        we get
                             |                           there?
         computers           |        activators
                          detail
```

mark HODGSON

The vertical axis of the model is about focus and ranges from 'detail' to the 'big picture'. The horizontal axis indicates 3 continua. 'past' to 'future', 'slow' to 'fast' and 'manage' to 'lead'. Stick with me and I'll explain. This creates 4 quadrants. Where should you be playing?

COMPUTERS

The bottom left quadrant. Detail-heavy tasks, based on current and past activity, are best performed by computers. Software, technology and artificial intelligence are now supremely capable at analyzing and extrapolating information for improving efficiencies. If you are spending a lot of time in this space, chances are you'll soon be replaced by a machine!

CUSTODIANS

Of course you do need to keep an eye on current business performance – at a big picture, strategic level. You must be in the 'now'. Here you are custodian of the business and the brand. It's about using your expertise and wisdom to maintain the status quo in a predictable, conservative manner. Shareholders and the market don't like surprises. The problem is that, for many, leadership stops here. It's necessary but not sufficient. Successful leaders must look, think and act beyond the present.

INFLUENCERS

Smart leaders have to build their influence. Influence is a new source of personal and organizational power. As the rate of change accelerates beyond our ability to keep up, we are looking for answers. We seek out the thought leaders who can tell us what will happen and how we can position ourselves to succeed. You will be future-focused, fascinated with creating the 'next'. You must cast off the shackles of conservatism and rebel. The future is likely to come from unexpected directions, so you need to challenge the status quo and push your thinking into new areas. You must also communicate your vision – to the business, to customers and the broader market. In doing so, you inspire confidence and attract new partners. This is where influencers create commercial advantage as the money follows the ideas.

ACTIVATORS

As exciting as the 'influencer' role is, it's not the complete story. The best leaders must also activate. That's about building the plan and resources to create the future you see. Making decisions. Switching from risk-management to risk-taking. Disrupting what already exists in the business and motivating and engaging the staff to want to go on the journey.

It's not enough to be a futurist with a helicopter view. Today's leaders must play in both the 'influencer' and 'activator' space – shifting between the big picture vision and the 'boots-on-the-ground' detail needed to bring it about.

WHERE ARE YOU PLAYING?

Are you focused in the past? Stuck in the slow lane? Merely managing people and processes? If you are in a leadership role, that's not enough. It may have been in the past, but not now. You are not creating enough value to secure your future. It's time to speed up, to become more agile, to look to what may be and stick your neck out in the process of creating it. There's risk of course, but leaders are in the risk-taking business. Better to fail-forward today than fail-completely tomorrow.

Playing in the wrong place almost caused the England rugby team to fail in what was meant to be their easiest game of the season. Ultimately, they adapted to the new paradigm and prevailed. They evolved and won.

Have you?

Discovering your second half hero

We had a lot of response to my recent blog 'Time to Jump – Launching your portfolio career'. I thought I'd follow it up with a companion piece that I wrote in 2015. It's about self-leadership. In it, I contemplate the forces that compete to either pull us back from or propel us towards finding a more purposeful version of ourselves. I call this our Second Half Hero.

I recently turned 50. As my wife Nicki also clocked up her half century *AND* it was our 20th wedding anniversary, we celebrated with a massive party at our local surf club. We had a fantastic live band, *'Fabulous Fifties'* theme and some very dodgy *'Diva Dad Dancing'*. It was also a great chance to catch up with friends. I was struck by how many of these conversations (those I can remember anyway!!!) arrived at the same destination. So many people were looking to change direction. Most had worked for several decades either for themselves or an employer, but few appeared to be fulfilled.

WEARING TWO HATS
This is a theme I also experience in my work with organizations. Invariably at the end of running a corporate leadership session, one or two people take me aside and quietly share an ambition to set out on their own. They are in the room wearing two hats – one as an employee and one as a would-be consultant, thought leader or entrepreneur. Whether this is a time-of-life theme or the result of increasing pressures and insecurity in the traditional employment market, it's clear that more of us are seeking to write a different ending. We're looking to do work that is more meaningful, work that fulfills our inner sense of purpose and that results in something we can be proud of. We are looking for what I call our **Second Half Hero**.

I NEED A HERO – BUT WHERE TO START?

Heroes come in many forms. From the comic book super-hero to the brave individual who steps up when others step out, or the driven visionary who selflessly creates something for others – perhaps a movement or a charity. In our own way, we all have an inner hero. The challenge is giving ourselves the permission to bring it out.

My model below captures the forces at play. We are wrestling with a complex combination of emotions and practicalities. On the one hand we have FEAR holding us in the past and unhappy present, yet HOPE pulls us towards our heroic future. On the other vertical axis, INERTIA battles with MOMENTUM.

Finding your Second Half Hero

```
                    MOMENTUM
                        |
        Disturbed       |    Purposeful
                        |
FEAR  ——————————————————+—————————————————— HOPE
                        |
          Small         |     Dreaming
                        |
                    INERTIA
```

FEELING SMALL?

In the bottom left hand of the model, we are both fearful and stuck in inertia. We feel that we are insignificant and failing. We're likely to be unhappy. We are doing nothing to move towards our better future. It is probable that we beat ourselves up with comparison to others – those who we perceive to be luckier, braver or more talented.

GETTING DISTURBED

It may sound counter-intuitive, but the best way to get out of *Small* is to become **Disturbed**. A useful energy can be found within the angst of Disturbance. It's where ambition to move forwards, towards our heroic future is countered by dissatisfaction with where we are. We begin to feel restless rather than resigned. To move on we need to commit to a positive course of action. We need to make decisions – some that will almost certainly involve taking on risk. Getting comfortable with risk is fundamental in moving us towards our more hopeful future.

DARING TO DREAM

If hope is the DNA of our heroic future self, we'd better have a dream. We need a vision of exactly what it is that we want to achieve or build. It's what will inspire us to action. Vision walls, sketches and bucket lists are all great tools that can help. **Dreaming** is necessary – but it's not sufficient. Hope without activity is just wishful thinking. To create energy around our vision we need to become focused and committed to a course of action that will turn our dream into a reality. We must commit to practical actions that start to connect our reality to our aspirations.

PURPOSE IS THE GOAL

When we have both hope and momentum we have a **Purpose**. WE ARE IN THE GAME. Purpose is the foundation for our Second Half Heroic self. When we have a guiding vision, a practical plan to fulfill it, support to help us and clear metrics around our progress, we are ready to achieve.

We may not have X-ray vision, the power to stop runaway trains or the strength to deflect earth-threatening meteors – but we do have something else. We have the ability to live in our purpose. Most people do not manage this. The tragedy is that most of us don't even try. I reckon we all owe it to ourselves to have a red-hot crack at first discovering and then becoming our Second Half Hero. The world needs us!

Time to jump – launching your portfolio career

I was recently invited to sit on a panel at one of Sydney's leading business schools to share my thoughts on how I had set up my successful 'expert practise' as a consultant. As I looked around, I was struck by the wide variety of people in the room. They ranged from twenty something students, presumably in the early stages of their careers, to folk in their 50s and 60s. Many had dropped in after work. It reminded me that there are many people looking to either start or transition into doing their own thing as coaches, facilitators, experts, entrepreneurs and influencers of one kind or another.

TIME TO JUMP?

So many of us are looking for this evolution. Drivers are many. Perhaps it's as a response to the decline in corporate job security, or a redundancy. Maybe it's people who are simply fed-up with corporate bullshit or who have a long-held desire to hang out their own shingle. I see these people everywhere. Frequently they approach me at corporate workshops for a quiet chat about the best way to 'transition'.

For many, it's likely this will be a blended or portfolio career, where one full time role is replaced by several different projects. This can be an exciting and satisfying evolution. A chance to spread risk and feed undernourished areas of interest.

5 YEARS ON

I've been playing this game now for around 5 years. I am getting used to it and have built a very successful business around my areas of expertise and interest. I now split my time between 3 key areas; 1. my work helping CEOs and their leadership teams transform themselves and their businesses, 2. my role as the Head of Consultancy at the brilliant About My Brain Institute and 3. my volunteer work as a Lifeline crisis support worker. I am now very comfortable, but it was not always the case. Prompted by my recent Q and A session, here are a few ideas that may be helpful if you too are thinking about taking the leap.

1. START EARLY

It takes a long time to establish yourself. However long you think it will take, double it. It took me two years to really work out who I was and to shift my thinking out of the old corporate mould. If you are in an organisational role, you can do a lot to prepare the path ahead whilst you still enjoy a predictable salary. So start creating content and publishing it into LinkedIn (more on this later). Attend networking events in the areas you are interested in well ahead of D-Day. Seek out people who are a few years into the journey and ask them for advice.

2. BEWARE THE BULLSHITTERS

Don't for a second underestimate how hard this transition can be. That's not meant to be negative or scary, but I have worked with a lot of people going through this 'journey'. Beware of get-rich-quick scammers spouting stories of overnight success. It's easy to think that everyone else is doing better and this can erode the fragile confidence of the first year or two. 'Out of the box' success does happen, but it's rare. And when you do hear of someone who actually launched a new coaching business and made $500k in the first year, you'll probably find that they were in a similar business before and had an extensive database to market their new offering to. For most people it's about patiently making connections and building a list. You have to understand who you serve, what problems you solve and then build your tribe. Doable? Yes. A quick win? Probably not.

3. ACT LIKE A STARTUP

In the tall ship sailing days, when the seas were rough, it was impossible to light the stoves. The sailors had to exist on hardtack – essentially longlife biscuits (you can make them here!). OK, you probably don't need to go that far, but you do need to wean yourself off corporate spending habits. However much you may think your employer has pulled back on allowances, flights and perks in the last few years, what you enjoy as a corporate is heaven compared to your new world as a solopreneur. Taxis, flights, meals, stationery, laptops – even your desk, chair and lamp will be paid for by YOU. As is your Super! Oh and you don't get a regular salary check of course, so it's likely you'll spend the first few months at least dipping into your savings. So make sure you have some! Think hipster minimalism rather than fancy hotel opulence. Don't worry, you'll get back to your 5 star finery if that floats you Boaty McBoatface, but probably not for a couple of years.

4. UNLEASH YOUR INNER CREATOR

This is important. When we work in organisations or study for Masters degrees in coaching and the like, we get very good at implementing other people's tools and ideas. This is great discipline, but it can also institutionalise our thinking. We've all seen the Shawshank Redemption movie where the old lags are so used to their confinement that they are unable to function when finally released back into the world. We can get a bit like that.

As independents the shackles are off. We can and must CREATE. Not only is it the best way to add value and build a point of difference in a crowded market, it's fundamental to our development and personal growth. It starts with giving yourself permission. You'll probably be fighting the inner voice of 'not good enough', but that will pass. The simplest way to start is to write a short blog like this and publish it into your LinkedIn profile. As I said earlier, you can and should begin this today – whether you are days or years away from your jumping off point. (Even if you are, like many, a very happy corporate, you should still be creating content – great for your career profile and getting that next promotion, but that's another blog). As my friend Matt Church is fond of saying, "just pretend no one is reading it". In the early days that will probably be true, but the habit of creating will over time help you to find your voice and to evolve the clarity and confidence in your message. By the time you have a tribe to sell to, you'll be in great shape.

5. BE PREPARED FOR THE MENTAL SHIFT TO NONAME.COM

Whether we are conscious of it or not, most of us are very attached to the status and sense of identity that comes with being Jo Schmo, Divisional Sales Manager of BIGCO. Within both our organisations and social groups, this is important. Who we are, what we have achieved (and probably what we earn) are readily understood. There is a great comfort in knowing our unspoken (but very well understood) place in the prevailing hierarchy.

Fast forward to Solopreneur land. You are now Jo Schmo from Noname Coaching or Jane Brane from MADEUPNAME that no one has heard of. This can be a real challenge. If you've relied for years on the brand identity of the well-known companies you've worked for, suddenly standing on your own can make you feel very small, almost naked. You'll also find that many contacts who love you for what you can do for them today will disappear. Be ready for that. Over time you will build the network of great people who will support you in your new world, but don't expect too many of your existing corporate contacts to step up beyond their own self-interest. Sad, but true.

GET HELP

There are many more things we could explore. I would recommend investing in a mentor to help you through the process. Of course, I would say that, as it's one of the services I offer. But, whether it's me or not, I think this is an essential. The transition can be challenging. It is easy to get stuck in periods of doubt and inactivity during which you earn little or nothing. When you consider the maths of living off your savings for months versus the cost of a good mentor and system to help you set the right course, keep moving forward and – perhaps most importantly – avoiding what can be very costly mistakes, it's a no brainer.

As someone who is now safely on the other side of the transition to a successful portfolio career, I look back across the chasm and encourage you to jump. The upsides far outweigh the negatives if you plan well, follow some of my suggestions here and, of course, work hard.

Part 2: Kick-starting thought leadership for your business

If you feel safe in the area in which you are working, you are not working in the right area.

Always go a little further into the water than you feel you are capable of being in.

Go a little bit out of your depth.

When you don't feel your feet are quite touching the bottom you are just about in the place to do something exciting.

— David Bowie

10 Reasons your company should embrace thought leadership

I just received the following blog post from Michael Henderson one of my partners in the Thought Leaders global movement. You can find out more about Michael at culturesatwork.com. As well as being an all round good guy, blessed with living on a small island in New Zealand's Auckland harbour, Michael is co-author of the *Thought Leaders book*. What follows is a great piece that lays out the real world benefits that you can gain from becoming a *'Thought Leadership Enterprise'*.

Without doubt the biggest growing topic clients have asked me about in 2011, was how and why their organisation should become a Thought Leader in their industry. What was interesting for me was that many of the organisations that approached me to discuss Thought Leadership admitted to not knowing much about the topic. The reason they were interested was that their clients were already underway becoming Thought Leaders, or were asking my clients if they had plans to provide Thought Leadership services to them.

The following is a quick overview of Thought Leadership and 10 reasons why your organisation should at least consider becoming known as a Thought Leader in your industry.

The term of thought leadership was first coined in 1994 by Joel Kurtsman, then the editor-in-chief for the magazine *'Strategy and Business'*. It was he who said that thought leaders are those people who possess a distinctively original idea, a unique point of view, or an unprecedented insight into their industry. A thought leader is more than just a subject matter expert who has unique insights or perspectives to share their area of expertise. Subject matter experts know. Thought Leaders are known. In other words a Thought Leader in your business is a subject matter expert who is well known in your industry as the go to expert on a particular topic. Their ideas are packaged in accessible and usually attractive formats, and distributed to a market that is hungry for their insights in direction and solutions to problems. The ideas that they offer are often powerful enough to shift or contribute to the future direction of an industry, community, or even a whole way of thinking.

10 reasons for your organisation to become a Thought Leader

1. Reduce the cost and time involved in generating new business.
2. Retain your best and brightest people through offering them development as a Thought Leader.
3. Position your organization in the industry as the Go to Experts, strengthening your brand and reputation.
4. Enhance information flow and retention throughout your business and across silos.
5. Position your organisation as Thought Leaders to render competitors' offerings redundant.
6. Enhance you employer branding – attract the best and the brightest talent from your industry.
7. Develop a powerful WHY for customers doing business with you other than product only.
8. Widen your market reach and relevance.
9. Enhance and re-invigorate your internal communications ability.
10. Build advocacy and brand loyalty through massively enhanced pro-active customer service.

Tools of our time

There's a famous scene in the prohibition-era classic *'The Untouchables'* in which Sean Connery (whose homogenous 'celtic' accent for once finds a home in his role as a gritty and long-time Chicago beat-cop) mentors his idealistic but naïve boss (Kevin Costner) on the realities of winning on the street with the now classic advice that you *"don't bring a knife to a gunfight"*.

The parallels for anyone trying to drive commercial success, either working for themselves or as part of a larger business are clear – you need to make sure you have the best tools to beat your competition to the business. In the *'new now'* markets, this means equipping yourself to maximise output and influence whilst minimising the costs of doing so – in other words, you need to become super-efficient. It sounds simple, yet how often do you see people get this wrong; think outdated powerpoint presentations, websites without videos, redundant hard-copy sales collateral and high-value, high-cost people performing low-value tasks in the age of the 24 hour virtual assistant?

In my gap year between school and university, I joined a small business that helped young Brits to get work at summer camps in America. Apart from myself, it was an all-female team. Fearing that I would attempt to treat my female colleagues as secretaries (remember this was the mid-80s), the first thing the manager did was to send me on a one week typing course.

At the time it seemed almost medieval, bashing away about *'the quack brown fix…'*. As a consequence though, I learned how to touch type (not brilliantly, but well enough) and as a result my productivity in today's world of laptops, e-books and blogs has sky-rocketed.

As with most things, you can take this too far and, certainly, it's easy to become horribly unproductive if you are forever chasing the latest 'silver bullet' killer app or shiny gadget. Likewise, we've all got lost in trying to be in too many virtual places at once and new is not always better. Doug Richards, TV Dragon and serial entrepreneur puts it this way – *"we don't need to be leading edge, but whatever our age, we do need to be current"*. This means we need to keep scanning multiple environments to see what might work for us. An efficient way to do this is to identify a small number of leading practitioners in your sector and follow what they are doing (and not doing!). Crucially, in a world of seemingly exponential change, we have to (cheerfully!) adopt an open mindset to avoid getting stuck in old thinking patterns. Failure to do so could see you coming second in a race where there is only one prize.

Permission to get PRODUCTIVE

I had a meeting with a client last week, a bright, energetic and enthusiastic young entrepreneur who wanted to convert her passion for creating beautiful, hand-made wedding invitations into a business.

The problem was that she was unsure of exactly what her offering was and so she had also started to branch out into a wider range of gifts and services for the wedding market (which I am reliably informed is still booming – every couple must have their special day, even in harder times!). She was slipping from a specialist to a generalist and losing focus. I gently pointed this out and she actually agreed. She mentioned that her web designer had also hinted the same thing. But how much more productive would it have been if at the outset of appointing a supplier (in this instance the web designer), she had framed the relationship by giving him permission to be 100% frank and forthcoming with his expert views?

There are three key components of the Thought Leaders teaching:

1. World-class I.P.
2. Clearly prescribed action plans.
3. An integrated suite of productivity tools and strategies.

Each one of these is vital in maximising income – not least the productivity piece that means we *'get more done more quickly'* (e.g. I am writing this on a train thereby maximising otherwise unproductive travel time – oh look, there's Tower Bridge).

Giving permission to those you work and partner with, to be open and honest with their advice or feedback is massively productive. It ensures you get the very best insights early and accelerates learning

and output. If it's advice you don't want to hear that's fine – better to learn your thinking is flawed or that a project is unlikely to get up early, so you can kill it and move on to the next thing.

The roots of this are complex and perhaps, as Brits, we are especially prone to being reserved and attuned to not cause offense. That's fine; and certainly, we shouldn't be ignorant or rude. The secret is in clearly framing the relationship from the get-go. I always ask clients for the permission to be completely frank with them. Of course they all say yes (I wouldn't work with anyone who said no – I simply could not serve them effectively) and we can then get super-productive, super-quick.

'The Five Dysfunctions of a Team' is an awesome (and wonderfully short!) book by thought leader, Patrick Lencioni. The primary dysfunction that underpins all others is the absence of trust and is fueled by *'the absence of open and honest debate'* – because it results in the 'group think' and false agreement that ultimately leads to non-ownership of results and poor performance.

Whether you are a solo practitioner or in a business of any size, give permission to those around you to *'get real'*. Frame it well, than stand back – enjoy higher quality debate and feel the energy levels and productivity sky-rocket as those around you are unshackled to contribute their very best.

Unleashing the entrepreneurs Inside your business

I am lucky to work with both self-employed and corporate experts. Not so long ago, it seemed as if larger organisations held all the cards. They had the scale and resources that enabled them to compete in markets and geographies that were completely inaccessible to the little guy.

In just a few years, those barriers have been torn down. Technology has leveled the playing field. Today, anyone with a half-decent web connection can compete from anywhere on the planet! To hold a video-conference used to require costly ISDN lines and high-end cameras. Now we can do it for free from our favourite café using a $300 smartphone. The high fixed-cost bases of larger businesses now weigh heavily. A new model is needed.

The future's already here – it's just unevenly distributed.

William Gibson

THE FUTURE IS HERE

The good news is that the model is already here. It's what the smartest self-employed consultants, experts and thought leaders have been doing since the technology revolution enabled them to play a much bigger game. They've become flexible, fast and frugal. I believe there are handsome commercial gains for the larger businesses that can emulate these approaches by creating their own internal entrepreneurs or *'employeepreneurs'*.

This is a challenging idea. Many will disagree and cite any number of reasons why this doesn't apply to them or can't be done. To them I say *"good luck"*. Here are just a few things I believe many businesses can learn from today's successful independents.

GET OUTCOME-FOCUSED

Working for yourself, you don't have the safety net of a monthly salary. It's brutally simple. If you do not get your stuff out and sell it, you starve! You have to *Think, Sell* and *Deliver* (repeat x 1,000). The flip side is you get very focused, very quickly. You don't have time for the unproductive meetings and other distractions that can make up such a big part of a corporate day. So banish complacency and stale *'norms'* by focusing on outputs and deliverables. What can you stop doing, shorten or accelerate to get more done, more quickly?

FAIL FAST

Not a new idea, but there is so much baggage around 'failure' in organisations (often despite claims to the contrary!). The small guy cannot afford to prolong a failed project. We learn, adapt, discard or tweak – fast. Failure must be de-politicised. It's a cost of doing business and a great way to learn and grow. Embrace, indeed celebrate, failure as an exciting and necessary part of the learning and earning process.

COLLABORATE

We need to move on from scarcity and control to develop an *'abundant mindset'*. Yesterday's top-down, triangular structures must be replaced by circles: communities and partnerships where knowledge, skills and resources are shared abundantly for a collective commercial gain. Speed trumps cumbersome structures and policies. This requires simplification and, above all, **trust**.

EXPECT THE BEST OF YOUR PEOPLE

People are extraordinary. It is incredible just how much the best information experts are able to create and sell using just a few support staff (physical and virtual) and leveraging the best available technologies. They are massively productive and very successful financially. By contrast, too many businesses concentrate on creating rules and policies designed around expecting the worst of their staff. So hire the right folk and then trust them to do great things! Equip them, inspire them and let them loose on the world!!!

HAVE SOME FUN
This may sound trite, but too many businesses I've worked in are joyless and dull. I've operated in lots of countries and many sectors and, without fail, the best business successes I've observed have come from teams and individuals who are fundamentally enjoying what they do! Unless your employees resemble Daleks, Zombies or Imperial Stormtroopers, a little laughter goes a very long way towards creating high performance. LinkedIn CEO, Jeff Weiner, captures this beautifully in his frank and witty *'people I most enjoy working with'* model.

AND FINALLY – GET ENERGIZED

Sitting across the top of all of these shifts is the need to tap into the ***personal energy*** of your staff. Traditionally it's what employees have been expected to park at the door as they put on their corporate mask (a bit like their *'telephone voice'*). It goes by many names – essence, enthusiasm, passion – and the businesses that can adapt to encourage their staff to bring it INTO the workplace stand to prosper exponentially.

I believe we are in the middle of an important shift. Many businesses I work with are already in the process of encouraging and resourcing their *'talent'* to be increasingly entrepreneurial and flexible. It's not easy and, at times not pretty. Significant change usually isn't. Get this right though and the rewards – personal, professional and organizational can be immense.

The C21 sales solution for a world that's stopped listening

Think, Sell, Deliver is the most important weapon in the Thought Leaders mantra box. We use it a lot when helping entrepreneurial consultants to grow from subject matter experts (outmoded and increasingly threatened by an omniscient Google) to thought leaders (relevant, valued and influential!). To maximise earnings and growth, we teach that time should be split equally between the three focus areas.

1. ***Think*** *(capture what we know)*
   Thinking always comes first. It's about capturing what we know and do, understanding what problems this solves and clearly differentiating the solutions we provide.

2. ***Sell*** *(connect our ideas)*
   We have always got to be connecting our ideas with the clients we help. We have to in-build this process into everything we do (and learn to love it too!)

3. ***Deliver*** *(master flexibility)*
   We have to brilliantly communicate of our ideas using multiple formats and media – workshops, videos, webinars, keynotes, intimate 1-on-1s, blogs, tweets et al.

BIG BUSINESS BENEFITS TOO
It's becoming clear to me that developing, a Think, Sell, Deliver, focus is an increasingly smart approach for larger businesses too. In fact, I believe it's an imperative. The corporate game has changed in so many ways of course, but I think the sales shift is one of the

most profound (and least understood). Specifically, the responsibility for revenue and new business can no longer rest with a small, discrete group – a sales team or a business development unit. As Dan Pink writes in his excellent book, To Sell is Human:

> *A world of flat organizations and tumultuous business conditions—and that's our world—punishes fixed skills and prizes elastic ones. What an individual does day to day on the job now must stretch across functional boundaries. Designers analyze. Analysts design. Marketers create. Creators market. And when the next technologies emerge and current business models collapse, those skills will need to stretch again in different directions.*

PROBLEM 1. NO ONE LIKES SALES

Does this sound like your business? My guess is not. Most remain structured around traditional functions (operations, finance, marketing, customer service, sales ……) – in other words, Pink's *'fixed skills'*. In my experience, few people are excited about having the challenges and accountabilities of sales added to their existing remits. In short, most corporate folk get as far away from sales as they can!

PROBLEM 2. TRADITIONAL SALES DON'T WORK ANY MORE

In the unlikely event that you do have a business chock-full of wannabe sales guns just waiting for the call, you've got a second problem. Sales have changed. Traditional sales and marketing *'push'* strategies are failing. Starved of time and overwhelmed with information, your customers are switching off to unsolicited approaches. Not only must more people in your business now sell, they (and probably a lot of your existing sales experts) have got to learn new ways to do it.

THE GOOD NEWS!

For those businesses prepared to think differently, there is a solution – and it's a good one. Successful companies can now build a *'pull'* strategy that attracts their target customers and partners. The best way to do this is to leverage the expertise of a whole cross-section of your staff to create the information and opinion that will help your clients to solve their problems. You can then connect this to your customer base though networks, meetings, blog posts, white papers, conference speeches, trade-articles and other touch points. It's effectively selling the skills, know-how, ideas and passion of your people. In a flat world this is all you really have to differentiate you from the rest.

This is what C21 sales looks like. It's *'pull'*, not *'push'*. The best thing is that, done well, it's something that anyone in your business can do and LEARN TO ENJOY! Mastering this approach builds a clear point of difference for your business and is a very smart commercial strategy.

How to avoid digital extermination?

It's 1993. In the classic movie, *Groundhog Day*, when Bill Murray is woken up repeatedly at 06.00, his technology is a radio alarm, an electric razor and a decidedly un-flat TV. With the exception of his razor, TV weatherman Murray is very much unplugged. Fast-forward 20 years, and the first thing most of us reach for in the morning (not going there!) is a smart phone, tablet or laptop – all packing more processing power than Apollo 13! Partly we need to know what we've missed while we've slept. Partly we need to re-join our unceasing battle with incoming information; an attempt to manage the over-whelm that is 24/7 connectedness in search of the nirvana of *'in-box zero'*.

We can reflect with a degree of longing for Murray's simple era of faxes, brick-size *'cells'* and pay phones. Today, we live in the land of digital mayhem. and now have to overcome so much more noise even just to begin a business conversation. The challenge is how to make ourselves heard in a world that's stopped listening and it's not easy.

So how do we stop ourselves being metaphorically *'exterminated'*?

C21 CONNECTION
At Thought Leaders, we reckon there are 3 things you need to do to *'be'* to cut through captured here in my model:

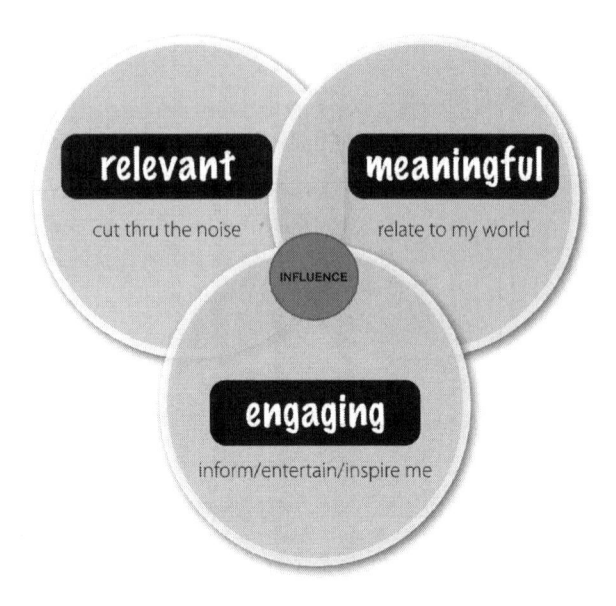

```
        relevant            meaningful
    cut thru the noise     relate to my world
                INFLUENCE
              engaging
         inform/entertain/inspire me
```

RELEVANT

Homer Simpson obvious? Perhaps. But so many of us forget to, first and foremost, be relevant. We need to establish why what we have to '*say*' is a priority. If we are not positioning our message as an answer to some of our customers most pressing needs, we are simply swiped or key-pressed into digital oblivion. Just reflect on how you treat irrelevant or low priority traffic!

MEANINGFUL

Once '*in*', we have to deepen the connection. Most of us are hanging on by the skin or our teeth trying to manage the sea of information we receive each day. We are strongly drawn to people we trust, like or respect – those who can simplify the 'noise' and create meaning for us. It's about empathy. In her wonderful blog, '*The Story of Telling*', Bernadette Jiwa recently wrote that '*Whoever gets closest to their customer wins!*' She's right and creating meaning is at the heart of it.

ENGAGING

'*Worthy*', '*solid*', '*academic*', '*extensive*' or '*robust*' alone won't cut it – at least in terms of grabbing the scarce attention of people whose default is 'NO!' If you're the Government proposing a new 20-year Defence Capability Policy for Australia you can do what you want. Suppliers will bend over backwards and wade through 800 pages of turgid prose all day. Most of us don't have that luxury. Our communications – emails, presentations, webinars, workshops etc. have to first seek to engage. They can do this by '*informing*', '*inspiring*' and '*entertaining*' our audience. Whatever the format – we have to earn the right to be heard.

A useful way to look at this is that we now have to think twice. Once about what we have to say (our message) and a second time about the best way to connect it (preference). Most businesses still don't do this well, meaning there's a ton of upside for those that do.

Time to put HR at the top table

IT'S THE PEOPLE STUPID!
Bill Clinton won his way to the Whitehouse on the back of a simple observation. *"It's the economy, stupid!"* He spoke the essential truth that fixing this one thing was paramount. His opponent (then President Bush) was campaigning on many other fronts (foreign policy, social policy, healthcare….) but Clinton's mantra cut to the heart of what was really going on.

In today's business, there's an equally obvious fact that many companies don't get. To paraphrase Bill – *"It's the people, stupid!"*. Whatever you do, chances are your competitive advantage relies overwhelmingly on the quality of your people. And if you don't have a competitive advantage, fixing up your people is the surest way to get one!

SO WHY ARE THE 'PEOPLE' PEOPLE NOT AT THE TOP TABLE?
Many organisations still position their HR Leaders at least a half rung down from the *'top table'* (CEO, CFO, CIO, COO and the like). They usually join *'marketing'* on a mezzanine level – just outside and beneath the *'real business'* conversation. Maybe it's because both *'people'* and *'marketing'* can be tricky to measure. That's true, but it's also lazy thinking. Getting both of these either very right or very wrong makes an enormous impact on the performance of any business. This needs to be changed – and it's up to you to do it.

TIME TO STEP UP
Lamenting the status quo won't change anything. These structures are hard-wired and unquestioned. If you want HR to take it's rightful place – *at the HEART of the business* – YOU are going to have to make the case.

Here are 5 ideas to get started:

RAISE YOUR PROFILE
You need to become a thought leader in your business. Start to contribute to the prevailing business conversation in a way that is engaging, passionate and authentic.

CREATE URGENCY
Build a program of great people projects with tight deliverables (90 days) to get your team excited, accountable and achieving.

JOIN THE DOTS
You need to continually show how great (and poor) people *'stuff'* directly impacts the more obviously measurable drivers. Talk up the $$$ benefits of great culture, high engagement and career path clarity.

PAINT THE BIGGER PICTURE
If you are to shift perceptions, you'll need to help others to re-frame the way they think about HR and 'people'. Help them to see. Tell stories that they can relate to.

THROW SOME ROCKS
Remember, we are trying to change the status quo. Don't be afraid to throw some rocks. Your vision, delivered with passion will be persuasive and not everyone needs to love it!

As an HR leader, you have the ability to create a framework that will encourage everyone in your business to reach their true potential. This is honourable work. Done well, it's also the surest way to get you the influence you need and deserve.

Time for a leadership revolution?

Across the globe it's been a tough week for establishment leaders.

ROYAL JESTER?
In Australia, Prime Minister, Tony Abbot has exposed himself to universal ridicule by bestowing a contentiously re-introduced Australian knighthood on Prince Phillip. It's hard to make a case for any non-Australian and particularly for the Queen's gaffe-prone husband who already enjoys a bewildering swag of titles. Will he even notice?

GREEK TRAGEDY?
In Greece, the old order has been swept aside with the stunning election victory of anti-austerity and anti-corruption party, Syriza, led by the charismatic Alexis Tsipra. How will it end?

THE DEATH OF COLONEL BLIMP
In Britain, the new head of Army, General Nick Carter announced his plans to cull a third of senior officers. Too many, he says, have gained promotion through *'good staff (or paper) work'* rather than inspirational leadership. He wants to create a new senior officer elite to lead a force that is *'agile, imaginative and effective'*.

CHANGING OF THE GUARD
There are many more examples of challenges to the old order finally becoming realized. The pace of change is quickening – agitated by economic inequalities and enabled by new mobilizing technologies. Fringe movements and niche player alike can now find a way to be heard. The game is up for out-of-touch leaders. In public life and in our businesses, we have come to expect more.

WHAT SHOULD WE BE LOOKING FOR?

Here are 5 key 'new-world' qualities that I believe successful leaders need to master. They must be:

Collaborative

We live in the ideas economy. Old positions based on scarcity and control need to be replaced by collaborative partnerships – perhaps with competitors. In the US, for example, electric car-maker, Tesla has just gifted a raft of its patents to the industry. This will enable competitors to catch up and help contribute to building the necessary infrastructure for e cars to cross into the mainstream.

Adaptable

Today's world is complex. Binary and inflexible positions and posturing no longer serve. Leaders must be able to flex and evolve with the situation.

Teachable

The shape of traditional leadership is a triangle. This reflects a fixed hierarchy with a solitary leader at its head. Today, it's probably a nebulous circle. In the world of VUCA where the world is *Volatile, Uncertain, Complex and Ambiguous,* no one can know it all. Leaders must be able to learn and build teams of people who know more than they do.

Authentic

We've run out of time and patience for posturing egos. Great contemporary leaders know their faults and are not afraid to name them (and work on fixing them up!) They are human and approachable. This is so important in getting genuine buy-in from your staff and customers.

Energetic

We all know the world is now '*on*' 24/7. The divide between work/home and professional/personal is, at best, blurred; at worst, non-existent. Today's leaders must be able to handle stress and bring a personal energy and enthusiasm to their work. They understand this *and* the need to build and nurture it through care and discipline around their fitness, diet and rest.

HOW DO YOU MEASURE UP?

This is a big ask for most of us. We need to work at acquiring new skill, mindsets and attitudes whilst also understanding what we need to retain. A lot of this is a departure from traditional business and leadership training. It won't happen overnight. The biggest step is in acknowledging that there is a need to learn and evolve our leadership skill set.

Once we've got that, we can change the world.

Time to get your people fully PRESENT?

It was 4.15 in the afternoon with perhaps an hour of daylight left when we arrived at Seal Rocks, a small beach hamlet on the NSW coast. After four hours of driving from Sydney, I was all set for a relaxing beer, but my son and his four 14 year-old mates had other plans. We had to go spear fishing – NOW! So off they went and, girded only by a reluctant sense of loco parentis, I grabbed my gear and followed them into the frigid-looking ocean…

… to be rewarded by the most extraordinary snorkeling adventure I've ever experienced. The water was in fact warm and as clear as gin. For the next hour I enjoyed a magical assault on the senses, as we swam over turtles, octopus, parrot fish, blue wrasse and a particularly impressive school (flock??) of Eagle rays the size of coffee tables. Left to my own devices, I'd have missed it all, but the excitement and sheer puppy-like enthusiasm of the boys was infectious.

ENTHUSIASM IS LIKE GOLD-DUST

Enthusiasm literally means, *"to be possessed of a God-like quality"*. I love this. It's why we are so attracted to enthusiastic people, those who are full of possibility, energy and can-do. I call these people fully PRESENT and, in the world of work, they are incredibly valuable. Problem is, we don't come across them very often. In fact, study after study tells us that the majority of employees are disengaged. They are physically 'present', but in every other sense, out to lunch – giving only a fraction of what they could. So how do get our people from *'present'* to PRESENT? My model below may help:

6 LEVELS of ENGAGEMENT

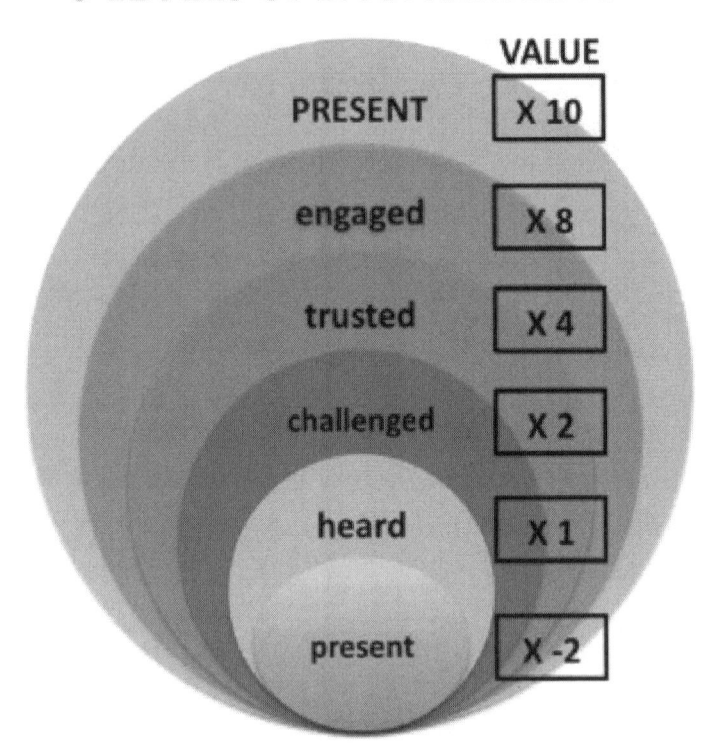

Level	VALUE
PRESENT	X 10
engaged	X 8
trusted	X 4
challenged	X 2
heard	X 1
present	X -2

Getting the best from your people

There are **6 Levels of Engagement** – each delivering a corresponding value to the business (and the individual). It's most obvious to think of the model as an aid to develop under-performing staff, but there's more to it than that. I believe it applies equally to the many managers struggling to adapt to generate the value they once did (and can again, with encouragement and a teachable attitude).

1. Present

This is the lowest form of engagement, where an employee

is only at work in a physical sense. I was dismayed to learn recently of a public sector organization where the only performance metric is hours attended (all 38.5 of them). There is no reward or encouragement for improving outcomes or increasing productivity (in fact it's informally discouraged). Staff who are merely 'present' are likely to be unhappy and probably costing you money. Better to have an empty seat than a completely disengaged body warming a chair.

2. *Heard*

To move your staff up the value chain, they need to feel they have a voice. Ask for their input on what can be done to make their job better or how they think things can be improved. Find out what's important to them. This is not to say you have to agree, but it's crucial to take the time to genuinely listen (and learn!). Once people are heard, their sense of unfairness or insignificance is at least reduced. They are more likely to at begin to add value to your business.

3. *Challenged*

I use this term in two senses. The first is to challenge people as in *"who goes there?"* At some point, every employee has freely accepted his/her role, presumably with a sense of excitement. In many of the corporate environments I've worked in and with, this simple truth gets lost. It IS absolutely appropriate to challenge employees who, once heard, are unwilling to develop a more positive attitude. No one is guaranteed a job and leaders must not avoid this difficult conversation.

More productively, people tend to react well to a positive challenge (as in, *"I challenge you to really give this a go"*). Good leaders challenge their people to grow personally to achieve more. Employees who respond to these challenge are now adding value and also likely to positively impact others.

4. *Trusted*
A natural outcome of the frank conversations at the challenge stage is the development of a deeper trust. If you can't or won't trust your people, something's very wrong (probably with you!). Once trust is established, people step up.

Autonomy is enhanced and decision-making accelerated. The value delivered can't help but be increased.

5. *Engaged*
With evolved levels of trust, sustained over time, results flow that are pleasing for both the business and the employee. Work is viewed as a positive place to be and a rewarding thing to do. These staff members are truly engaged and likely to be performing at 3 or 4 times the levels of the *'present'*.

6. *PRESENT*
At the highest level, your best employees will be fully present – bringing to the workplace the best possible version of themselves. They will be generating great commercial value, clustering into empowered teams and adding to a culture of high-performance, achievement and possibility.

TALENT FOR HIRE
Whilst you may not want to employ my son and his spear-fishing buddies just yet (5 teenage boys with spears – what could go wrong?), you'd love to have their energy in your business. I've found if you employ the right people and concentrate on enabling them to be energized, engaged and PRESENT the numbers that most leaders fixate on just take care of themselves.

Is your business too damn quiet?

We've all see films where, in an eerie quiet (typically just before all hell breaks loose), the hero says something along the lines of, *"it's quiet out there... too damn quiet"*. From John Wayne at *'The Alamo'* to Donkey in *'Shrek'*, it's a well-worn cinematic cliché. And whilst you don't want an invading Mexican army or a pitchfork-wielding mob running roughshod through your business, there's a good chance that a bit more noise could actually be a good thing.

WHY A QUIET LIFE CAN BE BAD FOR BUSINESS

For too long, we've been conditioned to minimize conflict in our workplaces. We prize consensus and agreement. Meetings are often about smoothing over differences or finding a compromise. Problem is that it's very easy to end up in either *'groupthink'* (where neither opportunities nor risks are fully explored) or *'false agreement'* (where dissenters stay silent – taught by bitter experience that *'resistance is futile!'*).

This may make for a quiet life and convey a sense of systematic progress, but chances are this *'peace'* is coming at a price. At best, you are missing out on the chance to truly harness the collective smarts of your people. At worst, you could be laying the foundations for under-performing individuals and failed teams.

WANT GREAT TEAMS – START A FIGHT!

In his excellent business fable, *'The Five Dysfunctions of a Team'*, Patrick Lencioni identifies five tiers of dysfunction, each negatively building on the other. The first of these is *Absence of Trust*. The second is **Fear of Conflict**. To fix this, he says we need to engage in *productive conflict*. In other words, we need to encourage our teams to have conversations that are passionate, energetic and possibly quite heated.

TIME FOR SOME CREATIVE ABRASION?
Harvard Professor, Linda Hill agrees. In her recent book, *'Collective Genius'*, she argues that to get the best from our people we need to in-build *'Creative Abrasion'*. We need passionate people from all levels of the business sharing their ideas, unfettered and unafraid. We need to be *ABRASIVE* – in a good way!

As Hill's model shows, to make this workable, we need two further elements: *'Creative Agility'* to test and refine the resulting ideas and *'Creative Resolution'* – which is a patient and evolving process that allows the best solutions to arise over time. Crucially, in this process the role of the leader is flipped. Their focus is on nurturing and maintaining the environment in which all of this can happen – not to be a central figurehead who sets the vision and leads the charge.

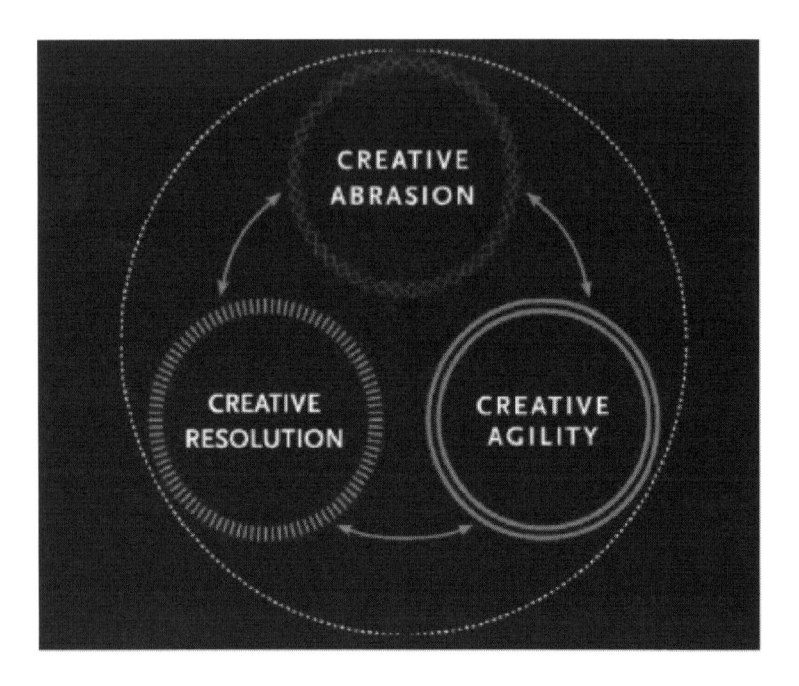

CREATIVE ABRASION

CREATIVE RESOLUTION

CREATIVE AGILITY

WHAT'S HAPPENING AT YOUR PLACE?

Do your corridors and meeting rooms resemble a library? Are raised or animated voices heard or encouraged? Is there a sense of creativity, energy and occasional friction?

These are good questions to ask. The social norm is very strong. We are conditioned to polite order. Whilst I'm not condoning rudeness or aggression, I do think there is a lot of upside in encouraging our people to be more energetic and unfiltered in expressing their ideas. Yes, it will raise new challenges. You will need to positively manage this new dynamic to prevent negative excesses. That done, I believe the upsides will far outweigh potential negatives.

3 great ways to put thought leadership to work in your business

It's finally happened. Thought Leadership has gone *'mainstream'*. How do I know? **LinkedIn** has created *'The Sophisticated Marketer's Guide to Thought Leadership'*, a great summary on why smart businesses need to get across this. As someone who has been immersed in this space for many years, I think it's a great document.

UNLOCKING THE MYSTIQUE

One of the challenges is to make thought leadership attractive and accessible. This shouldn't be hard. It's simply about attracting more customers to your business. It makes you money, grows your people and enriches your culture. For a long time, however, thought leadership has been misunderstood. Many businesses have placed it in the 'too-hard' basket because they can't see the value or don't know where to start. The **LinkedIn** piece breaks down thought leadership into 3 categories. I think this is helpful in providing businesses with a *'way in'*.

3 WAYS IN TO THOUGHT LEADERSHIP

1. Product Thought Leadership

This is a great starting point for any business. It's explaining in a neutral and easy-to-access way how your products solve the problems that your customers experience. It's about sharing best practise and *'how-to's'*.

The tone should be one of generosity. Do your best to provide great information that will genuinely help existing and potential customers. There should be no expectation of immediate return. Crucially, do not sell from this place. *Any business of any size can generate immediate commercial returns by getting involved in product thought leadership.*

2. **Industry Thought Leadership**
   This is perhaps what most people think of as *'thought leadership'*. It's about getting the experts inside your business to share their thinking in a way that will contribute to or shape the development of your sector.

   You will comment on the news and pick the trends and forces shaping your market. The aim is to position your people (and therefore your business) as a leader and a thinker. So challenge sacred-cows! Throw some rocks! Future cast. Then show the way by mapping out the path that will get people from the status quo to where they need to be.

   Industry thought leadership is very powerful. Few organizations do this well or consistently. I believe it's a high-ground that, in many cases, is there for the taking. Smart leaders who understand the commercial merit of playing this game will do well to plan their assault on the summit!

3. **Organisational Thought Leadership**
   The last category has an internal focus. It is better suited to larger organizations and can be summed up as a content-marketing strategy for your staff and customers. Using a wide range of communication channels (e.g. video, workshops, facilitated staff or customer sessions) it can bring your values, vision and culture to life. It's about the promotion of ideas, encouraging participation in debate and empowering innovation.

   Organisational thought leadership can be a very effective way of energizing the structures and dynamics that exist in larger organizations. For a very low investment, this activity can result in greater levels of staff engagement, contribution and therefore business performance.

NO LONGER JUST A 'NICE-TO-DO'

Thought leadership has been around for over 20 years. It has always been a good thing to do. What's changed, is that it's now an imperative. Traditional sales and marketing strategies are failing and we need to do different things to stand out and exert influence. Thought leadership is a big part of this. It costs very little and there are no down sides. In truth, there's no good reason for every organization not to be exploring the possibilities in at least 1 of the 3 approaches.

WHY LINKEDIN?

An indication of this growing importance is that LinkedIn has produced their white paper. It's done as a promotional activity for several of their properties, including the recently launched **LinkedIn Influencer** program – a channel tailor-made for showcasing thought leadership. When the world's largest professional networking portal creates a specific platform for this kind of information distribution, you know it's a mainstream event. You sit on the sidelines at your peril.

GETTING STARTED

So time to get going. Task your experts to create some content, book a slot to speak at your next industry event or make some *'how-to'* videos. It may be a bit rough at first, but that's fine. Any journey worth making starts with a few small steps. The trick is to start at all!

Developing your resilience 5-pack

Whatever line of business you are in, chances are you've never experienced a more competitive environment than today's. To be at the races, let alone in the winner's enclosure, we all need to do more with less and more quickly. The once clear divide between our personal and profession lives is now a fuzzy blur. Busy execs and time-strapped entrepreneurs are just as likely as gaming teenagers to be busted for breach of the 'no devices at the table' rule. Like politicians stretched by the 24/7 news-cycle, we too can find ourselves overwhelmed by the need to create, connect and communicate – stuck in an exhausting *'always on' mode – all 'enabled'* by new technology.

Whether we have to do these things, or, mistakenly, just think we do, it's very easy to get overwhelmed. These heightened expectations are not going away. Part of our success story must therefore be to manage our personal resources and energies so that we can consistently perform without burning out. In a word we need to become more RESILIENT.

Build your Resilience 5-Pack

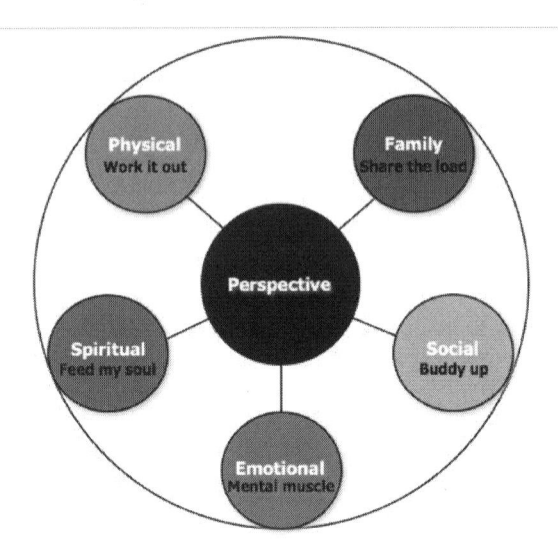

Diagram: Five circles (Physical – Work it out; Family – Share the load; Social – Buddy up; Emotional – Mental muscle; Spiritual – Feed my soul) arranged around a central circle labelled "Perspective".

EQUIPPING OURSELVES FOR ADVERSITY

I've created a model that captures the essential elements we need to first recognise and then balance to maximise our resilience. It's based on the thinking behind the US Army's *Comprehensive Soldier (and family) Fitness programme*. The genesis for CSF was the Army's frustration with the very high number of combatants who were returning from war theatres with post-traumatic stress disorder (PTSD). The traditional response was reactive – i.e. treating the sick. Very few preventative measures were in place. Research indicated that soldiers were often over-reliant on a few pillars of strength for their overall wellbeing (typically physical fitness, and sense of belonging to the army unit – Physical and Social in the model). Once these are undermined by exposure to the stresses of war, it becomes almost inevitable that PTSD will follow.

A Positive psychology approach has since been developed and implemented across the entire US Army. Simplistically, it encourages soldiers to develop a broader range of strengths on which they can draw to retain balance and wellbeing in times of adversity. So rather than standing on a two legs, we instead create greater stability by developing five! I call this the Resilience 5 Pack!

IT'S ALL ABOUT PERSPECTIVE

Whilst we're not soldiers, I believe that the same principles are just as valid for over-stretched staff. It's about recognising and developing strengths in five areas of our lives – Physical, Family, Social, Emotional and Spiritual.

Physical (work it out). Pretty obvious, but so many of us don't do this well. Whilst we are not about to go *'over the top'* into a hail of bullets, keeping ourselves physically fit is important to keeping our energy high. We need to exercise and balance our diet. I run and swim regularly – a great way to clear the head.

Family (share the load). They may drive us crazy on occasion, but family trumps all. We need to value those who are close to us. I know I've got this out of whack at times in the last couple to years. A good way to re-focus is to answer that golden question – *"what's my why"*.

Social (buddy up). Get out, get a life. Socialise outside of work. It's really easy to consign this one to the *'not enough time'* basket. I play rugby mainly for the social element (and the beer). It's great to chew the fat with a bunch of guys who have nothing to do with my day to day (or high quality rugby!).

Emotional (mental muscle). Make no mistake, the pressures of managing ourselves to deliver against a multiplicity of demands and expectations (from others or ourselves) can take a very real emotional toll. We need to find a way to feed our emotional strength. I have a few male friends who I can confide in and share with at a deep level. This works for me, but counselling or other strategies are great too. I think the thing is to name this as a need that must be met – not label it as a kind of weakness.

Spiritual (feed my soul). A very personal one, but, again, worth naming, addressing and nurturing. I am a Christian and I know I get great strength from this – especially on the tough days. Like the other 5 strengths, I have to work at it. When I do I know that I am better at what I do.

Perspective sits in the middle of everything. To maximise our resilience, there is nothing better than taking the time to know where we are:

1. ***In relation to others.*** The vast majority of people on the planet will always be worse off than anyone reading this. Losing a sale, missing a plane or staring in horror at *'the blue screen of death'* is not the world's biggest tragedy!

2. ***In relation to ourselves***. Run a health check around these five pillars. What are you doing well – what do you need to fix up? Score yourself out of 5 for each and put in place 3 actions to top up any area in which you are weak.

Mastering Resilience is key to achieving and maintaining our success – whatever that means for you. We are not sprinters – we need to condition ourselves for the longer haul – to suffer the slings and arrows and still turn up the next day with a smile!

Are you scarce or abundant?

Recently I ran a programme in Darwin in Australia's Northern Territory. I stayed at the *Hilton*, which at $180 a night is a pretty decent hotel (in fact good enough for Tony Abbot, the Aussie Prime Minister who was staying a few doors along – something I can't imagine happening in London or Washington?). Imagine my shock then when I was told that in-room wi-fi cost an additional $27 per day!

I was offended. My client was paying and, I am sure, would not have even questioned this expense, but I opted to use the 8 hours of free wi-fi available – to anyone – in the lobby. I figure that Paris already has plenty and I didn't want to rip my client off.

ARE HOTELS A BUSTED MODEL?
Hotels then are trapped in a *'scarcity'* mindset. It assumes we have no choice and will – albeit reluctantly – allow ourselves to be ripped off. Their problem is that we no longer live in scarce times.

As customers, we are now more informed than ever and – enabled by new technologies – have choices (e.g. make cheaper calls from our own smart phones or access free public wi-fi networks).

Their persistence with this approach means that a typical customer experience is really poor. I've paid a lot of money already and yet, for a few low-cost items, I am again and again asked to pay.

I feel, at best, cautious and, at worst, royally ripped off (something I'll be sharing with the world on any number of social media outlets).

SO WHAT'S THE ALTERNATIVE?

We live in a time where businesses need to adopt an *'abundant'* attitude. It's about giving more to get more. In his excellent book, *'Free'*, futurist Chris Anderson writes that;

> *Sooner or later every company is going to have to figure out how to use Free or compete with Free*

Chris was talking about completely free alternatives to paid models (such as free but limited versions of software that we get to like and then upgrade to a paid *'premium'* version – e.g. LinkedIn or Evernote). With hotels, they don't even need to be free, just way smarter in the way they charge. In my Darwin experience, I know I'd have felt completely different if the room rate was say $20 dollars more and included FREE wi-fi and FREE soft drinks. I'd have gladly paid this (remember I did not pay a penny over the $180 because of my poor customer experience). I think most other guests would have too. The hotel would have a lot more happy customers – delighted by an *'abundant'* hotel experience AND increase their profit due to the low real cost of a few cans of lemonade and a bit of data.

IT'S ALREADY HAPPENING

In London, the *Hoxton Hotel* near Old Street is pioneering this kind of thinking. It's a classy hotel in a chic location, yet all calls (including international) and wi-fi are free and the room rates are flexibly priced so that the earlier you book the less you pay. In the face of new competition like *Airbnb* – the *Hoxton*, like many other hotels knows that it has to offer a different and better customer experience. The traditional pay-plenty-as-you-go model is heading for extinction.

Unlearning the corporate vanilla

So you've decided it's time to get noticed, for your key people to step out in the marketplace. They are going to make a noise, *'zag'* when the herd is *'zigging'* and create disruption.

We believe that there is no better change strategy to create a vibrant and positive positioning for your business. You don't need to be the biggest or best resourced, you just need to be creative and a little brave.

Your people need to be bold, to tear down a few sacred cows, to throw rocks at the big guys (in fact we encourage exactly this strategy!). This is not about being needlessly sensational, rude or contrary, it's about offering your unique take on what's going on in a way that clients will notice and value.

One of the toughest parts of this transition is to unlearn corporate speak. As an ex-corporate myself, I know how, over time, we learn a politically correct, expedient and bland language, shaped by a complex array of cultural, habitual and even legal forces. We become vanilla, beige and diluted. To break the mould, we need to change. We need to be double chocolate, fire engine red and triple strength.

Here are 3 quick steps to re-discover your authentic voice and create messages that matter:

Shape – test with clever industry outsiders
Sharpen – find the essence; 3 big ideas, 9 slides
Shift – does it radically challenge the status quo? If you run these across any of your major external (and internal!) communication pieces, you'll soon find you've kissed goodbye to the corporate corduroy!

Old gold

My 14 year old son has just *'discovered'* David Bowie…

Like most of you, I didn't know he was lost, but '*We can be Heroes*' is the *'new'* cool anthem for the kids on the Northern beaches of Sydney. Similarly *'hot'* tunes are the *Phil Collins* drum intro' on *"I can feel it in the air tonight"* and *Mark Knopfler's* iconic guitar riff on *Dire Strait's* classic, *'Money for nothing'*. Everything old is new it seems – at least to some – and I must say I think it's brilliant. In an obscenely wasteful age that worship's everything on the altar of *'new shininess'* (iphone 6……7……8……whadeva!) it's great to see that we've not thrown out everything for the crime of being more that one version *'old'*!

BIG HAIR AND COLGATE SMILES
I was also reminded of this by a recent visitor from the old country. He was packing a dog-eared copy of a very *'80s'* business book by Mark McCormack. Paul is a sales pro and made the comment that, whilst over 30 years old, there was a lot of great insight still to be found in the yellowing pages. I checked it out and he's bang on the money.

WISDOM FROM AND FOR THE AGES
This got me started on a little journey back in time. Below I've grabbed some favourite observations from thought leaders of yesteryear; Mark McCormack, Peter Drucker, Niccolò Machiavelli and Marcus Tullius Cicero. I love them – what do you think?

Mark McCormack – on business smarts

1. Never underestimate the importance of money. It's how business people keep score!
2. Never overestimate the value of money. Cash is important, but sometimes not as important as respect, thanks, integrity, or the thrill of a job well done.
3. You can never have too many friends in business… Given a choice always do business with a friend. It's the best way to leverage your success.
4. Don't be afraid to say, "I don't know." People will respect you much more and will always place more weight on what you do say…because they know you're right.
5. Speak less… No one ever put their foot in their mouth when they were not speaking. Worse, if you are speaking, you can't be listening, and we always learn much more from listening.
6. Keep your promises, the big ones and the little ones…both the starting point and the staying point in any business relationship is trust…not suspicion. Someone who does what he says he will do will always succeed over a person who doesn't keep his word.
7. Every transaction has a life of its own… Some need tender loving care, some need to be hurried away.
8. Commit yourself to quality from day one… It's better to do nothing at all than to do something badly.
9. Be nice to people…nice gets nice, and all things being equal, courtesy can be very persuasive.
10. Don't hog the credit…share it. People will work with you and for you if they are recognized. They will also work against you if they are not.

American lawyer, sports agent and writer. Founder of the

International Management Group. 'The 10 Commandments of Street Smarts' (1989)

Peter Drucker – Oh genius man. Elegance, brevity and unparalleled insight

1. *If you want something new, you have to stop doing something old.*
2. *There is nothing quite so useless as doing with great efficiency something that should not be done at all.*
3. *What gets measured gets improved.*
4. *Meetings are by definition a concession to a deficient organization. For one either meets or one works. One cannot do both at the same time.*
5. *Management is doing things right. Leadership is doing the right things.*

American writer, management consultant and university professor (1990s)

Niccolò Machiavelli – all you ever need to know about change!

There is nothing more difficult to take in hand, more perilous to conduct, or more uncertain in its success, than to take the lead in the introduction of a new order of things. Because the innovator has for enemies all those who have done well under the old conditions, and lukewarm defenders in those who may do well under the new.

Italian historian, politician, diplomat, philosopher, humanist, and writer during the Renaissance (c. 1500)

Marcus Tullius Cicero – A life lesson for us all!

Being and appearing grateful is not only the greatest of virtues, but the parent of all others.

Roman philosopher, politician, lawyer, orator, political therist, consul and constitutionalist. (c. 50 BC)

I think we can all learn a lot from re-visiting these and other classics. They may be old, but they are very, very cool. Sadly, I don't think my son will still think the same about Dave, Mark and Phil's legendary songs once he finds out that his mum and I like them too!

Get more customers by offering less

THE POWER OF OMISSION

Offering your customers less, not more choice, can be a very smart strategy. The *ALDI* supermarket chain will be familiar to both UK and, increasingly, AU readers of Pinch. Relative newcomers to an Australian market heavily dominated by *Woolworths* and *Coles* (combined market share 72.5%), the German value chain again recorded record growth to take 10% of the market in 2013 (Roy Morgan Research).

There are a couple of reasons for this meteoric rise in a very mature and uber-competitive market. One is value. A typical basket comparison offers savings of 20–30% – not to be sniffed at in an age where frugality is the new black. 95% of products are little-known, but – crucially – high-quality alternatives to big brand offerings. So *'cheap'*, NOT *'cheap and nasty'*.

The second reason is that *Aldi* stocks around 10% of the 15,000–18,000 lines of a 'full-service' supermarket like *Woolworths* or *Sainsburys*. Not only does this help *Aldi* achieve fantastic buying economies, I believe it also attracts shoppers overwhelmed by options who value the simplicity of the *Aldi* shopping experience.

Instead of 10–20 choices of tea, ice cream, spices and meat cuts, *Aldi* customers are offered a binary experience. Spaghetti – white or brown. Milk – full or lite. Sauce – brown or red?

TOO MUCH CHOICE IS EXHAUSTING

I first visited Moscow when I was 18. Communism was at its height. The shops offered little and the locals had pretty much zero choice (though bizarrely, non-Russians could buy a wide range of western *'luxury'* goods in special hard currency shops). Back then, the idea of unbounded choice was seen as nirvana.

Fast forward to 2014. We are *'over'* choice. There are options everywhere and for everything. Just think of the permutations around ordering a cup of coffee (especially in Melbourne, where they take these things seriously!). It used to be *'black'* or *'white'*. Now it's a shopping list – size, type, strength, heat, milk type, froth, topping… Each option asks us to make yet another decision. We've become overwhelmed by choice and it's exhausting.

MURDER YOUR DARLINGS!
To maximize our own value with clients, we must employ this principle when we go to market. Invariably when I am helping my clients to sharpen their *'message'* it's a case of editing and reduction. It's often a painful process. We have to leave great ideas and options on the cutting room floor. An advertising friend calls this *'murdering your darlings'* – the ideas you are in love with that you feel just HAVE to be in your offering. What is left is a clear and concise argument, powerfully made.

1. Mr/Mrs client
2. This is what is going on (Context)
3. This is what I (your trusted expert) think about it (Concept)
4. This is how I know (Content)
5. This is what you need to do (Prescription)

As thought leaders it pays to offer this mixture of authority, conviction and prescription. It's so much more powerful than offering a menu of options, which places the choice back on the customer (who is seeking answers, not more questions) and detracts from your position as the expert authority.

So time to commit murder?????

Add some strings to your bow

MID LIFE CRISIS IN RED

On the way to my first coaching session of the year. Sydney's roads are deserted and I am cruising along on my stunning fire engine red motorbike. I glide across the city from the beautiful Northern Beaches (known locally as *'God's* country and for good reason) bound for the hipster quarter that is Surry Hills. Sun's out. Feeling good. Over the Harbour Bridge, lovely right-hand bend in front of the Opera House and take the slip at Woolloomooloo (yes, really).

A BUMP IN THE ROAD

Hmmm – that's not quite right. Suddenly the back end feels a bit squirrely. Something is up. Or, as it happens, down. Rear puncture. Bugger! My laid back vision for the day deflates in sympathy. No spare on a motorbike and years of experience prepare me to expect a lengthy and expensive wait for a man in a van. I'll inconvenience my client and have to re-do the whole thing. Grrrrrrr – some start to 2015.

THE LIFESAVER

I reconsider though. Travelling at a glacial pace, I can still move. The roads are super-quiet, maybe I can get away with it. Yes, I'm only a couple of clicks from the café, and I get there on time and enjoy a great session. There's a tyre garage next door! They don't do bikes, but direct me to a place just up the road. Things look up again as I limp along deserted streets usually crammed with impatience. I make it and meet Anthony, my new best mate. *"Let's have a look"*. *"Nah, haven't got one in that size mate, but can put in a string for you"*. I nod, as if I know what that is. Turns out, it's a temporary repair that get's my day back on track. Anthony diligently drills a hole and does clever things with rubber! I look on from the café next door (Hipster of course!). One cappuccino later – job done.

Just 90 minutes earlier I thought I was going to be down over $1,000 in lost business and recovery costs. But I made my session and now Anthony has patched me up. I'm good to go on to my next meeting and only out the cost of the repair. *"How much do I owe you?"*

"Nothing mate, I don't charge for strings."

I am speechless. Anthony has spent 15 minutes sorting me out with no expectation of payment. He's saved my day. We keep chatting and I end up booking in my bike for a needed service and two new tyres. It's across town from me, but with a bit of juggling, I can make it work for both of us. That's probably worth $3-400 profit to Anthony, but it only came about because of his generosity. You see this was not some slick marketing gimmick, like a loss leader. It was utterly authentic. I reckon he just knew that over time if he helps blokes like me that good things will happen. And he's right. We can get deep and talk about the psychological principals or reciprocity, but we don't need to. In a world that has become so calculated and measured, it's a delight to find a genuinely helpful business. When we do, we love 'em to bits.

WHAT'S YOUR 'STRING'
My question? What are you giving away without expectation? It's got to be genuinely valuable and something you know will really help your customer. Perhaps it's a free *'health check'* consultation (that is NOT a pushy sell in disguise). Maybe it's a webinar or a *'how to'* video series. Maybe it's that when it rains at your outdoor cinema experience you hand out brilliant ponchos for free (rather than exploit a captive market to make a few extra bucks). Take a

bow St George Open Air cinema.

The ability to genuinely surprise your customers can be priceless. So add a *'string'* or two to your bow and see what happens.

Time to get on the radar people

TIME UP FOR THE LUCKY COUNTRY?
I write this week's *'Pinch'* from seat 20C, returning to Sydney after running my **Blog or Die** content creation program, in Adelaide with my good mate and fellow Thought Leaders mentor, Rod Buchecker. It was a great day and our students left on a high – full of fresh insight, inspiration and know-how to help them stand out from the crowd by sharing great content that their market will love. Looking at this morning's newspaper headlines, the timing for them is perfect. You see Australia has finally run out of luck.

THE HANGOVER
Most lottery winners end up penniless. They become overwhelmed by a seemingly inexhaustible supply of cash, splurge it on all the wrong things (assisted by new *'friends'*) and find out too late that the smart play is to preserve the lump sum. Australia has enjoyed an extraordinary resources boom over the last decade, but instead of seeing it for what it is – a boom that will sooner or later 'bust' – successive governments have instead acted like a student with their first credit card. Falling demand from China and an iron ore price that has crashed by 40+% are clear signals that the party is over. And it will affect all of us as governments cut services and business sentiment sours.

BOOTCAMP HURTS!
Tougher times mean tougher competition. More then ever we need to invest in a strategy that will help us to stand out in. I see too many people playing it safe. Given the potential storm that's coming (and we only need to look to Europe and the US to understand the *'BOOTCAMP'* levels of pain involved in turning around out-of-shape economies), *'safe'* is, in fact, a really bad place to be.

TIME TO SHINE

So what to do? My job is to help clever people be commercially smart – and the smartest thing we can do in the face of this challenge is to bring 'all of us' to our game. We need to shine.

As my model shows, there are 3 elements to who we are. Trouble is most of us have spent a lifetime trading on just two of them – our Expertise *(what we know)* and our Experience *(where we've been)*. Think of your resume, your Linked In profile or the *'About XXX' bio'* piece on your website. Chances are it's full of your academic/professional achievements and your employment track record. Great for establishing your credibility, of course, but no longer enough.

[Venn diagram: Expertise (what I know), Experience (where I've been), Essence (who I 'be'), with overlaps labelled credibility and conviction]

COULD THE REAL YOU PLEASE STAND UP!

Think of who is really making their mark in your business or sector. I bet they are passionate. I bet they move you with the power of their belief. I bet you sense that they are utterly authentic. In other words, they've captured their Essence *(who we 'be')* in the way they turn up professionally. That's the key to standing out.

So time to stick your head up and get on the radar! It's a smart response to tougher times. It's also extraordinarily rewarding. You'll probably lose a bit of paint on the journey, but trust me it's worth it.

Is your expertise ready for the big time?

I've just returned from a great family holiday to Nashville, USA. I'd never been there before, knew very little and – accordingly – had few expectations. Well, let me tell y'all (as they say there) the secret's out. Nashville is going off! In the last decade it has positioned itself as a significant artistic and commercial destination. It's the cultural capital for both kinds of music (country and western!), has it's own NFL football team and is the home to some of the largest healthcare businesses in the world. Hipsters abound. Known as Music City, it is THE go-to place for every musician looking to be discovered as the next Dolly Parton, Kenny Rogers or Johnny Cash.

TALENT IS NOT ENOUGH
Downtown Nashville is full of Honky Tonks. In and around these bars, musicians by the score rotate through stages – large and small. Unpaid, they are literally singing for their supper.

For those not lucky enough to get onto even this tenuous stage, there is the street. Here, numerous, fiddlers, singers and even drummers ply their trade. Now that's commitment!

All of these performers are super-talented. Nashville is no place you go to unless you can "play pretty good". But it's clear that only a very few can ever make it. Talent alone is not enough.

FROM EXPERTISE TO INFLUENCE
It's the same for experts in the business world. One of the greatest challenges is adapting to stay commercially relevant. That can mean staying in a job, or getting good work as a consultant or

entrepreneur. Many of us grew up in a world where the formula was expertise + time = success. We studied hard, earned academic and professional qualifications, joined at the bottom of an organization and – with hard work, time-in and a bit of luck – gradually ascended the ranks.

If we're honest, we know the game has changed. The value of our expertise and experience is diminishing. How rapidly depends on the industry sector, but, in a time of technological revolution, business model disruption and dizzying advances in artificial intelligence (to name just a few), we need to re-think how and where we add value.

UNIS ARE PIVOTING TO STAY RELEVANT

As a reflection of this, several universities now offer MBAs specifically for entrepreneurs. The premise is no longer to enable graduates to land a bigger job. Instead it's to fast-track the development of the business nous, networks and entrepreneurial skills they'll need to fly – probably in their own start-ups. In the UK, a different twist sees Universities offering an apprenticeship-style degree. Here academic studies are integrated with real-world businesses as part of their development (think Oxford University goes TAFE!). All of this is about developing people who don't just know stuff, they also know how to collaborate, connect and innovate to get things done.

That's all good for new players, but what about existing experts like you? The market for traditional specialists is highly competitive. Just like in Nashville, there's more supply of than demand for talent. So how do YOU stand out?

UNLOCKING YOUR UNIQUE INTELLIGENCE

I work with a lot of smart people and help them to cross the gap from subject matter expert to influencer. There's a lot to it. At its heart though, the secret is to understand that your 'uniqueness' is a blend of several qualities that combine to form your UQ. My UQ model explains:

Your Unique Perspective (UQ)

- **Expertise** — what you know
- **credibility**
- **conviction**
- **Experience** — where you've been
- **Essence** — who you 'be'
- **authenticity**

Expertise (**what** you know): Clearly, you need to 'know' something. This will be your main area of knowledge and an area in which you will have worked hard at developing over many years.

Experience (**where** you've been): Thought leaders maximise their influence by the size of the problems they solve (not the amount of time they spend solving them!). Their unique insight is based on their own experience of doing things well – or, just as often – what they learned from getting it wrong. Theory, however evolved and elegant will only take you so far. This is where the new MBA and blended apprenticeships aim to add value. It's at the interface between Experience and Expertise that we establish our all-important **Credibility**.

Essence (who you '**be**'): To build your reputation, people have to like hearing what you have to say. We can all think of unquestioned experts who leave us cold with their poor presentation or lack of clarity. You must become a good (better great!) communicator – to connect your ideas with skill and passion. Essence combines with your experience to demonstrate your **Authenticity** and with your expertise to build that compelling sense of **Conviction.**

IT'S NEVER TO LATE TO GET DISCOVERED

You may have heard of the inspirational story of Sixto Diaz Rodriguez. After a brief musical career in the US in the 1960s he faded into obscurity and lived a meager life in Detroit. In South Africa, his records – particularly the hit 'Sugarman' – and his popularity lived on – completely unknown to Rodriguez. An unlikely chain of events eventually led to him being rediscovered in the last decade. He finally made it!

My point? There's hope for us all! Most of us need to do more to move out of the false comfort of our expertise. We need to develop our UQ. It is available to everyone. Yes we need to commit to moving into new places of learning and vulnerability. Yes, it is likely to be challenging. But when we do, we're a chance. Whether we are the drummer by the trash can or the lead guitar in the Honky Tonk, we may just be on the verge of greatness!

Think twice to maximise your influence

It's been one of those weeks. Running around like the proverbial fly, continuously aware of a ticking clock... get to the meeting ... tick; send that proposal... tick; make those calls... tick; fill up the car... tick; pick up X from Y... tick...

We're all juggling time. There are still only 24 hours in a day, yet, by necessity (and also choice), we try to squeeze in more and more. Most of us fail. The result is half-done tasks, half-read books and half-hearted conversations. We adjust by making decisions about what we give our time.

WHEN 'DELETE' BECOMES DEFAULT
Like many, I start the day by de-cluttering my inbox. Before I'm even out of bed, 80% of overnight emails have gone. As aspiring influencers, we need to think about the best way to make our ideas attractive enough to avoid digital oblivion.

WE NEED TO THINK TWICE
Part of the problem is that we default to norms. Email is convenient, so we use that. Powerpoint slides are engrained so we use those. There's nothing wrong with either, but we make a mistake by using them unthinkingly. A voice call, an invitation to walk and talk, coffee at an interesting location, a bespoke video pitch may all be better ways of getting attention and results.

We need to think twice. First about what it is we want to communicate and second, about the best way to do it.

Think Twice to Maximise Your Influence

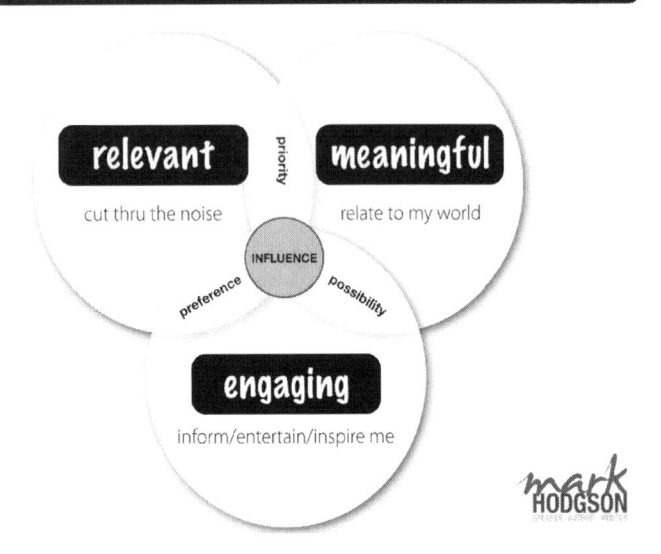

relevant — cut thru the noise
meaningful — relate to my world
engaging — inform/entertain/inspire me

priority · preference · possibility · INFLUENCE

mark HODGSON

Whilst there are no guarantees, there are three hoops to shoot for. It we can connect with some or all, our chances of cutting through are greatly enhanced.

1. BE RELEVANT

Think about your own filtering process. What goes, what stays? In a world of many things and people competing for our time, only the most relevant things remain. Anything from a boss tends to capture our attention of course. So too do things we think will address our most pressing problems. We need to make our ideas a priority to have the best chance of cutting through the noise.

2. BE MEANINGFUL

Nothing kills attention faster than dry, impersonal content. Most business-speak still defaults to numbers, metrics and other 'left-brain' information. We need to tell the 'right-brain' story that brings it to life. We must personalize the data to mean something important in the world of the recipient. So a 5% increase in profitability is great. But a 5% increase that has enabled the business to make a $10,000 contribution to a charity that my team selected if we hit our numbers is magical. It moves me emotionally and makes me feel that what I do counts!

3. BE ENGAGING

The last thing we'll make time for is stuff that bores us. Be brave. Get your ideas across in a way that informs, entertains or inspires. Use great images. Tell a story that makes your point. Use humour to crack the tension. Anything that you can do to defuse the 'formal' business paradigm will help. It may feel safe, but it's ineffective. The more authentic and informal you can be, the greater the chances that your message will land.

BUILD YOUR INFLUENCE

There's no shortage of clever people or great ideas. Knowing stuff is great, but it's not enough. May of the people I work with come to me because they are frustrated at their inability to sell their expertise. Rethinking the way we communicate is the first step.

Standing out in the gig economy

It's all sweet in the 'Gig Economy'. These are the findings of a recent EY report, *'Is the gig economy a fleeting fad, or an enduring legacy?'*. Also known as 'the contingent workforce', the Gig Economy is where businesses contract talent on a short-term project or even a daily basis to deliver their services and expertise.

The practice is not new. What's changed is the scale – largely prompted by the focus on costs control following the 2008 GFC/Recession. Businesses love the savings of only paying for what they need when they need it, rather than carrying the costs of full time employees. With many former corporate workers, freelancers and consultants seeking greater variety and flexibility, there is a ready, able and willing supply of experts on tap.

EY Report key findings:

50% of organizations have seen an increase in their use of contingent workers over the last five years.

By 2020, almost one in five US workers will be contingent — the equivalent of 31 million people.

55% see contingent workers as helping to control labour costs.

50% believe contingent workers can help to overcome resistance to change within the legacy workforce.

42% are using contingent workers to respond to seasonal workforce requirements.

Inevitably, the rise of the Gigger has seen a steady decrease in full time jobs. Even Australia, which boasts a low headline unemployment rate of 5.9% (Jan 2017, ABS), is experiencing a decline in full time jobs (down 40,000 yr/yr, ABS). It's not hard to see why. Giggers are not only flexible, compared to full time workers, they're cheap! They don't attract super contributions, sick pay or annual leave. With the true cost of a full-time employee estimated at 136% of their salary, you can see the attraction. Great talent on tap at the right price.

EVERYONE'S A WINNER?
Whilst there would seem to be scope for giggers to feel aggrieved, EY's report finds that, for now at least, the experience is positive:

> *56% of giggers agree that contingent working is how they want to progress their career.*

> *66% believe the benefits of contingent working outweigh the downsides always or most of the time.*

My view is that this will change. The Gig Economy is a human version of technology-enabled disruption. Like many of these markets, early participants are excited by the new possibilities. Over time however, returns diminish as more resources (in this instance people) become available.

Airbnb gone flat?
We recently put a granny flat onto Airbnb. We've been watching the market for a while and it's clear that we're not alone. Supply is exploding as others also see the possibilities of deriving rental income from underutilized space. If you remember your high school economics, when supply increases and demand stays the same, prices fall. The gold rush may have passed.

Uber drivers taken for a ride?
In Melbourne recently, Uber drivers went on strike in protest of the over-supply of vehicles and low effective wages (as little as $11/hour). Former evangelists now see the downside of a completely flexible, agile model where nothing is guaranteed. They are now seeking better conditions and a minimum wage (like taxi drivers!)

THE BOSS KNEW
As Bruce Springsteen sang in pre-digital times, *"you don't work and you don't get paid!"*. That's the rub with all of these models. An empty airbnb room, a stationary Uber driver and a Gigger who ain't gigging all earn the same – nothing.

A RACE TO THE BOTTOM
There are of course benefits from the Gig Economy, but I think it's best treated with caution. Newscorp recently made most of its photographic staff redundant – only to re-hire many of them as freelancers. This is a good example of the business imperative to gain access to talent on a flexible, low-cost basis (and damn the ethics!). Great for the business – but for the Gigger?

THE COMMODITIZATION OF WHITE COLLAR JOBS
There's little downside for organisations in transferring as many roles as possible to the gig economy and the EY numbers support this. Everyone's doing it right? And as the supply of Gigger talent increases – following the uber and airbnb examples – it's likely that the day rates will fall. We're already seeing this with the rise of agencies like Expert 360 and ICG in Australia. These match organizations with the experts they need on a project basis (e.g. CIO, CFO, Change lead). Models vary, but Giggers are invited to tender for a gig and the best 3 selected are forwarded to the client at a predetermined price for final selection. Not my idea of income security or fun.

YOU NEED TO STAND OUT FROM THE CROWD

The gig economy is here to stay. It makes sense to play in it, but only on your own terms. That means making it part of your career portfolio mix as a consultant, expert or entrepreneur. But relying on it for your future – even if current levels of reward appear attractive – is high risk.

It's far better to build your own position as an influencer and thought leader. That means creating a clear position in the market – who you are, what problems you solve and who you help. Next you build a personal brand around that and obsess on communicating with power, empathy and elegance.

In a gig world, investing in building your personal brand is a smart way to stand out. Indeed I reckon it's essential. You'll be hard to pidgeon-hole or commoditize. You'll attract your own customers and command the high prices your talent deserves. You can still pick up the gigs that fit, but you'll be in the driving seat.

Why it's OK to play the fool on the hill

I've always loved the Beatles. As I explored in 'Bringing out the greatness in others' the variety of their music was extraordinary. For me, it's their quirky songs that stand out; none more so than *'The Fool on the Hill'* – a song about a scarecrow.

Day after day alone on the hill,
The man with the foolish grin is keeping perfectly still,
But nobody wants to know him,
They can see that he's just a fool,
And he never gives an answer,
But the fool on the hill
Sees the sun going down,
And the eyes in his head,
See the world spinning around

In literature, the 'wise fool', is a well-known archetype. It's probably best seen in the many fools William Shakespeare created to impart wit and wisdom, often to show up the ignorance of their superiors. Puck in *'A Midsummer Night's Dream'*, Falstaff in *'Henry IV'* and The Fool, in *'King Lear'* all exist to tell us what's really going on.

STANDING OUT CAN FEEL FOOLISH
In our own way, we too must be fools. The journey to becoming a successful influencer often starts with more of a whimper than a bang. In setting out new ideas, new approaches and challenges to the status quo, we're often seen as wacky, off-piste or just plain wrong.

In his excellent TED video, entrepreneur Derek Siver captures the intricacies. It's spot on, funny and short. Just 3 minutes to convey an essential truth on how to start and build a following.

GET COMFORTABLE WITH VULNERABLE
Siver's argues that anyone wanting to start something new will, at first, risk the ridicule of looking like a *'lone nut'*. That's about standing strong in conviction, but completely unsupported by anyone else. If you've ever been the first person on the dance floor you'll know the feeling – especially if your 'moves' are of the 'Dad' variety like mine!

STAND IN YOUR CONVICTION
There's no question that *'first mover'* can feel like a tough place to be. Worse, we may have to stand there for months rather than the few seconds in the video. Is it worth it? I think it has to be. Aspiring influencers need to have a bit of the lone nut in them. (This is why being a thought leader is SO much more than being an expert. They are NOT the same thing). If we want to stand out, to attract new followers and make money, we need to experiment. We've got to put it out there.

In a world of same-same products and services, there's never been a greater need for businesses to innovate. There's also never been a greater prize for those souls brave enough to stand out. As we gradually build a following around our ideas, we also grow our confidence, our income and our legacy!

Maybe it's cool to be the fool after all? Hope to see you on the hill!

Part 3: Creating a winning mindset

If everything seems under control, you're just not going fast enough.

— Mario Andretti

Don't die wandering

A funny thing happened at the weekend. Through one of those weird friend of a friend of a friend deals, we arrived at the unexpected privilege of offering a bed for the night to a remarkable young photographer passing through Kent called Mihai Tufa.

Mihai, 26, is by his own admission, relatively inexperienced with the UK being the only country he has visited outside of his native Romania. Not the obvious launching pad then, from which to shoot for Mihai's goal – to walk around the world. Yes, the world. That's 100,000km (*just* 62,000 miles in old money!) and an estimated 7 years of his life. He thinks 8 people have already achieved this extraordinary feet (!). To put this into context (and we love context at Thought Leaders), more men have taken *'one small step'* on the moon than the one hundred million give or take needed to circumnavigate this planet earth that we all call home.

Will he make it? I don't know, but I certainly hope so. His biggest fear is that he will *'die wandering'* – freezing to death in the Russian winter, self-barbecuing in central Australia or being eaten by a grizzly bear in Alaska – take your pick. What I do know is that just by setting this outrageously *'hairy'* goal, Mihai will grow and increase in ways that he can't possibly fathom today. He might die wandering, but he won't die wondering. Even if he falls short of such an audacious ambition, he will surely arrive at a better place than if he never set out.

The biggest failure point for most of us in achieving personal freedom (in time, money or any other currency that we value) is our own limiting belief. We either don't set goals at all, or those that we do set are so modest that they don't move us forwards sufficiently quickly to change our paradigms.

My point? If a young, relatively inexperienced young man from one of Europe's poorest countries believes he can walk around the world, what's stopping you?

You get What You Expect

There's the old story of the shoe salesman who is sent to a new overseas market. After only a week he phones his boss and tells him it's useless. *"I need to come home. No one here wears shoes"*. A second salesman from a different company goes to the same market and after a week call his boss – *"send more stock, no one here wears shoes"*.

Our own attitude and mindset frames our expectations. I was reminded of this recently when travelling around London and listening to the radio. We Brits are famed for being world-class complainers and certainly, we'd be set fair for a massive medal haul if there were events for being anti-the London Olympics. Objections range from the capital will be paralysed by traffic, the traditional tourist trade will be decimated and of course, all the best tickets have gone to *'the rich'*. So are we set for 2 weeks of *'living hell?'*

I was fortunate enough to be in Sydney prior to the 2000 Olympics and remember a lot of the same concerns. There was talk of mass exodus *'for the duration'* and employers having to make special arrangements to keep their businesses running as the privileged purred past in their luxury cars in special *'Olympic lanes'*. It was all going to be terrible. And what actually happened? For two weeks, the city was transformed in what became a celebration of all the very best aspects of humanity – not just the obvious triumph over adversity stories of the athletes, but the tremendous spirit created by spectators (physical and virtual) and the thousands of volunteers that in turn infected even the most skeptical to become part of the celebration. For two weeks we talked to formerly unknown neighbours about the nuances of events we knew nothing about and shared a thousand stories of our own little adventures.

For two weeks we were transfixed – glued to every new unfolding story. It was a truly wonderful time.

My prediction is that exactly the same will happen in London. We will host a wonderful games and, for two weeks, this extraordinary city and its extraordinary people will shine. My point – if you believe this and speak this, it will happen. Just as in your business, if you believe and speak in can-dos, positives and amazing possibilities, you will also find that you may be calling your suppliers to *"send more shoes"*.

You can't get ahead by following the crowd

I've set myself the challenge or writing this week's pinch in the time it takes to get back to base on the train from London. 24 minutes (or so the timetable confidently trumpets). Productivity, productivity, productivity!

In our quest to become the go-to experts in what we do (making more money and having more fun along the way) we need to stand out, to differentiate and to create a valuable point of difference. Fact is, we can't get ahead by following the crowd. We have to be prepared to challenge the status quo, to shake it up and to trial our ideas and hunches. We have to take risks.

A great way to do this is to challenge customer expectation – to use our expertise to tell them about the big problems that they face (and you solve) that they perhaps can't yet see or appreciate. I call this their *'unknown problems'*.

I've spoken to a large number of small business people recently and most tell me their problem is cashflow, cashflow and cashflow. Whilst technically true, for many I suspect that their bigger problem may be indecision. Great decisions + action = focused activity.

Focused activity tied to discrete projects creates the energy, purpose and momentum that in turn drives business performance and profitability. Great productivity generates great cashflow! Not always true, but you get the point.

Of course, you've got to handle your approach carefully. Your customers probably won't like to be told they are wrong. But if you can help them to see their world from a different perspective – to show them what's really going on – there's every chance that you will impress them with your insights. You'll stand out from your competition by demonstrating your thought leadership in a really practical way that clients will love, value and buy.

What are you missing?

THE MOVE
Twenty years ago in the dark of a Budapest winter, my wife, Nicki and I were up to our eyeballs in the second of our many moves around the Hungarian capital. We worked there in the late 90s and first lived in a beautiful apartment building overlooking the Danube (as seen today in every European river cruise TV ad). Grand, chic, glorious; but no longer what we needed following the arrival of our first child, Izzi. Time to move *'across the river'* to the Buda hills.

THE *'VALUABLES'* BAG
So it was *'on'*. We didn't have too much *'stuff'* back then and were moving ourselves. The drill was to carry our boxed-up life across the internal courtyard, down the stairs and out to the roadside ready to be packed into the car. Any rubbish we'd also place in the bins outside. We had a *'valuables bag'* of course. This was where all the most important items lived – keys, money, passports… For reasons I can't now recall, this was a bright yellow *'Duty Free'* carrier bag.

JOB DONE
At last, we were finished! We carried down the last few precious items – the cat, the valuables bag and our newly minted, beautiful 6 month-old daughter – rugged up like an Eskimo! We loaded, said our fond farewells to a very happy home and drove the 30 minutes to our new *'out of town'* house.

AN UNPLEASANT FEELING
We arrived, tired but excited. A new chapter. Unpacking could wait until tomorrow. We'd just relax with a bit of TV. No problem,

just need to find the satellite card – it's in the valuables bag. I'll grab it…

Can't find it.

"Nicki, do you know where the valuables bag is?"

"No, I thought you had it"

"I thought you had it!"

The search starts. As we look, look again and then again, I began to experience that terrible sensation that starts in the very pit of your stomach. That dawning realisation that something is very wrong. Can't find it anywhere. Frantic now – I head for the car. SURELY we haven't mistaken it for rubbish and left it by the bins….

Of course, we *have*. I arrive to find the remnants strewn outside our old home. Time lessens the pain, but we had lost our passports, birth certificates, wallets, credit cards, marriage certificates and around $US4,000 in cash – the first month's rent. Ouch! The lucky finder had also scored a couple of chilled *'celebration'* beers and a day-old copy of the London Times! Our only wish is that it was a true blessing to whoever wondered across the spoils of our oversight whilst rummaging through the bins.

STRESSED BUT UNBROKEN
Nicki and I are celebrating our twentieth wedding anniversary this year, so we obviously got over our loss and, even at the time, we put it down to experience. We'd both ASSUMED the other had packed the bag. As the old saying goes, it had made an ASS out of U and ME.

WHAT ARE YOU ASSUMING?

We all fall into the habit of assuming. We assume we know what our customers want. We assume that what's worked in the past will work again. We assume that our staff are motivated because they once were…

We assume because it saves time. We assume because it's easy. We assume because it saves us from thinking. But thinking is what we now need more than ever.

In his excellent new book, *'What do to when it's your turn'*, Seth Godin expands on the opportunity we all have to step up and make a difference in today's *'ideas economy'*. Everything has changed and so must our thinking.

It's a call to action. A call to question our individual and collective assumptions – to re validate, reject or extend their relevance. It's a challenging, even scary exercise. But the rewards from aggressively deconstructing our assumptions can be both personally liberating and commercial dynamite.

So let's all have a try. I just hope that your assumptions aren't costing you quite as much as some of mine.

Are you inspired by the company you keep?

Just a few weeks into the year, I'm already excited by the new people, ideas and communities I am discovering. Are you?

TEACH TO LEARN
They say the best way to learn is to teach. Every day, I am learning from the fantastic people I mentor. It's such a privilege to help smart people from a diverse range of experience dedicated to exploring, pushing and commercializing their expertise. They even pay me to do it!

GROW OTHERS TO GROW OURSELVES
At another level, in my role as a business consultant, I recently interviewed an inexperienced young lady for the role of receptionist. She had not done well at school and – in the absence of good advice – had made a few poor job choices. But she came across as tenacious, imaginative, and hard-working. She's a superstar in the making – just waiting for someone to believe in her. I know she'll grow as part of an exciting business that will provide her with support and opportunity. I am so thrilled that her life course just got supercharged because she had the gumption to apply for a job on SEEK. I am inspired by the chance to help.

SEEK OUT MEANINGFUL NETWORKS
At a community level, in late February I'll be at the Thought Leaders Business School quarterly *'immersion workshop'* in Sydney. It's a coming together of the clans, chock-full of seriously interesting, successful and energetic people all committed to developing their commercial thought leadership. Over three days, we'll review progress, share learning and map out targets for the next quarter.

Trouble is there are so many great conversations to be had in so little time that I typically only manage a handful of the many that I know I will enjoy. That's what happens when we surround ourselves with inspiring individuals.

ARE YOU INSPIRED BY THE COMPANY YOU KEEP?

Whether you work for yourself or an organization, this is a great question to ask? If you believe (as I do) that we need to be in a state of continual growth and learning to succeed today, a good place to start is by connecting with excellent people. But how many of us do this well and consistently?

WALKING BACKWARDS INTO THE FUTURE?

Too many, I fear, are missing out on the value of great company – stuck instead in tired conversations and repeating patterns. I've recently sampled the trade press *'dialogue'* in two fields that I used to work in, only to find that the conversations are the same as they were five and more years ago. That's not good enough and certainly not commercially smart. As thought leaders, we need to be looking forwards, elevating the conversation and pushing the boundaries (and buttons!) of the status quo.

WHO CAN HELP?

Here are some ideas about what to look for in the people you want in your tribe. They should:

Inspire us

First and foremost, they must interest and motivate us. Inspiring people feed our own energy and help us to see how we can grow.

Mentor us

Find someone who has already achieved what you want to. Ask them to mentor you. How did they go about it? What mistakes did they make? How can you learn from and serve them?

Challenge us
One of the most valuable aspects of the TL Business School is that it provides an environment in which we can overtly challenge each other to *'do the work'* of thought leadership. The world is full of excuses and the journey is hard. When we're surrounded by focused people (who will not accept the easy way out), we are driven to achieve – in a good way.

Encourage us
The flip of this is that we will stumble. Projects will fail, we'll get discouraged and have our mettle tested in many ways. The right people will encourage us through these inevitable, but temporary, setbacks.

Do you know these people?
I hope so. If not and you feel stuck in tired and predictable conversations, it's probably time for you go out of your way to find them. This may involve moving out of well-worn (worn out?) relationships. It will probably take some effort. The reward though may well lay the foundation for something remarkable.

Why courage is essential in our Brave New World

My favourite time of the week is when I volunteer as a Water Safety swimmer for the weekly Nippers sessions at my local surf lifesaving club. Nippers teaches kids age 5–13 how to safely enjoy the surf. One of the key activities is the swim. 100 metres off the beach we set a buoy and simply swim out and back!

Of course, there's more to it than that. There are distinct zones. Each requires courage to enter. Most kids are comfortable in the shallow water inside the waves. But to get to the buoy, we need to go out of our depth and swim towards the breaking waves. This can be daunting for the kids (and indeed many adults). At 'the break', where the waves crash into us, there are cries of "over" or "under" as we decide which way to keep moving through the roaring walls of water. We are fighting the fear of being out of our depth, being smashed by the waves and of venturing further into the ocean. Logic tells us that the further 'out' we go, the greater the danger. Instinct tells us to turn back to 'safety'. But we teach the kids to "swim hard". You see, once you are beyond the break, everything changes. The water is calm. The rips are gone. It's a beautiful place.

I usually swim with one of the less confident kids, helping them to keep going – out of their depth, through the break and, finally, out the back. We 'high five' the buoy – our Everest! As we do, I always get the kids to look back – to see how far they have come. Their sense of achievement is wonderful. Courage is rewarded!

This is a metaphor for so many facets of our lives – at home and work. In a competitive and stressful world, we too must strive to achieve. We too need to get to the buoy! We need to be courageous.

*Either you decide to stay in the shallow end
of the pool or you go out in the ocean.*

— Christopher Reeve

COURAGE IS NOW A LEADERSHIP ESSENTIAL
Courage is one of the four pillars of the Collaboration Competency in the i4 Neuroleader model:

Inspiration
Communication
Generosity
Courage

Courage refers to the ability of a person to face difficult circumstances despite being fearful. This includes not just physical challenges. It's also about having the fortitude to say what needs to be said, understanding when and how to do so and also accepting what cannot be changed.

In turn, *Courage* is made up of three elements:

Fear Management
Ability to Redirect Efforts
Trying New Things
Fear Management

In the centre of our brain, two small structures called amygdala are believed to control our fear responses. New research suggests that other parts of our brain also play a part. Given how big a part fear can play in our lives, how we can influence these mechanisms is the subject of much study.

From a leadership perspective, the fear drivers that perhaps keep us alive in a survival context can be misplaced 'at work'. Defensiveness and other reactions can damage relationships and affect collaboration.

The SCARF model, developed by Dr. David Rock identifies five domains: Status, Certainty, Autonomy, Relatedness and Fairness. Each can be a trigger for our fear-based reactions to people and situations. Awareness of these is a good start when thinking through interactions and leading in a way that minimises the threat response.

ABILITY TO REDIRECT EFFORTS
When things go wrong, looking at the bigger picture, working out a new solution and redirecting efforts while letting go of self-doubt depends on an inner ability, called 'self-efficacy' – a term coined by American psychologist Albert Bandura. In our ever-changing and unpredictable world, this is a powerful leadership quality.

Self-efficacy is a new paradigm. Older leadership models often employed a much more fear-based element, using secrecy and punishment to maintain 'control'. Relying on threats and consequences is an ineffective approach – particularly with younger workers. Flipping this, accepting failure as a necessary and valuable part of the contemporary business process is far more effective. Believing in your people and resourcing them to perform is smart business. Fear-based strategies just don't work in our agile and unpredictable environments.

TRYING NEW THINGS
Many managers get stuck in repeating patterns. They try to solve

today's problems with yesterday's approaches, often misunderstanding how the context has shifted. These habits are often embedded in culture and processes, making it hard for new ideas to be tested. Breaking this cycle takes real courage. It's the courage to take on the status quo, to go against often more senior naysayers and to influence those around you to also step into the unknown. To date, neuroscience has few answers to how we can offset this inhibitory process.

As leaders, we must work hard to bust this cycle. It is the essence of leading change. It requires us to understand that each team member is likely to have a different response to change. We need to be intelligent about how we encourage and challenge, but we also need to be persistent. Succeeding in our VUCA world is largely about how well and quickly we can create change-agile teams. That's people who relish a challenge and are able to experiment and adapt to opportunities and threats with a smile. A great way to develop this capability is to set a vision and inspire action. As Dale Carnegie observed.

> *Inaction breeds doubt and fear. Action breeds confidence and courage. If you want to conquer fear, do not sit home and think about it. Go out and get busy.*

COURAGE TAKES MANY FORMS

Courage is a new leadership currency. It is complex. We need to summon our courage and then think how we can best deploy it to generate the team and business outcomes we need. It's also deeply personal. It calls on our emotions and vulnerability. As Dr Brené Brown said,

> *In one of its earliest forms, the word courage meant "To speak one's mind by telling all one's heart." But this definition fails*

to recognize the inner strength and level of commitment required for us to actually speak honestly and openly about who we are and about our experiences – good and bad. Speaking from our hearts is what I think of as "ordinary courage".

Drive success by being yourself

Have you noticed how many successful people have a knack for making their life look a little less bumpy than yours. They appear to glide across life's challenges, unfazed by the everyday dramas that conspires to frustrate your progress. If your dream is to make a great living selling your expertise, this lightness of touch can seem both attractive and inaccessible.

IT'S NOT LIKE IN THE MOVIES

Would that we could live in the unreality of the silver screen. There's a lot less friction. In Braveheart for example, Mel Gibson manages to deliver the mother of all pre-match team talks to thousands of very angry, very blue Scots. Not a "pardon" or "sorry we didn't quite catch that at the back" to be heard. Russell Crowe did the same in Gladiator and recently, Daenerys, our favourite G.O.T. Dragon Queen was inspiring an entire city from the top of a pyramid. Look, no microphone! Meanwhile, in the real world, I struggle to hear from the other end of a table for 6 in a busy restaurant.

GOT A TARDIS?

Likewise, travel and parking is never a problem. Exhibit 1. – a typical episode of The Good Wife. The love-hate-love law partners slide effortlessly between office, court, office, home, court, restaurant, lover's home, office – like Time Lords. No sweating on a parking spot. No cursing cancelled trains, planes and meetings. Back on my planet earth, I've recently been wrestling with an incontinent cat, digital castration courtesy of the recent Sydney storms (movie title, Broadband Down!) and had to interrupt a client call to help my daughter remove a very large spider from her car. Sound familiar?

KEEPING IT REAL
The point? We've all got our own drama going on. A big part of the challenge of moving from our present into a successful future is to function in our reality – to succeed in spite of these petty (and not-so-petty) irritations. I'm coming to believe that the secret is to actually embrace and share the drama rather than pretend it doesn't exist. Let me explain.

DROP THE FACADE
The good news is that we can drop the act. In fact, we can even improve our appeal by acknowledging that we live in a real world full of distractions, fears and unvoiced priorities (like getting to our kid's swimming carnival). There has been a shift. We no longer need to pretend that we have all of our shit together or that we are something we're not.

SMALL IS COOL
Time was when businesses would only do business with established suppliers with their own city offices. Now, many companies understand that some of the best minds are working on their own or as part of small collaborative ventures. Their 'offices' may be the local coffee shop or a converted garage. And that's OK.

EMBRACING OUR TRUTH IS POWERFUL
One of my Thought Leaders colleagues, Christina Guidotti, is a master of empathy. The first thing she does in a workshop is to share her story. She talks about her family, her aspirations, mistakes she has made along the way and what she has learned from them. Then she asks the students to do the same. It doesn't feel very 'business-like', but it's stunningly effective. Posturing evaporates. Platitudes crumble. Real problems quickly surface and we get to work on solving them. Being vulnerable, personal and authentic is in fact very smart business.

THE PEOPLE WHO MATTER DON'T MIND

Of course there are still many customers who will only buy old-school. That's fine. They will never work with you. What's important is there are more than enough who 'get' that your ability to solve their problems is far more important than your office address. They value your expertise, productivity, agility, speed and 'Get Shit Done' mentality more than the formalities of a business charade that is well past its sell-by date.

That's great news. To succeed we no longer need to be micro-versions of established businesses. We can be well-rewarded and still get to do the important things in our world. And if we're a little ragged around the edges occasionally – who really cares?

Getting over our 'Manshit!' to make a difference

I thought I'd share the 'match report' email we sent to the mighty men of the Newport Nasties over-35s rugby team, following our run/swim/fun event this morning in support of RUOK? Day. You don't need to know us to know people like us in your world. We had fun and – who knows – maybe saved a life.

Suicide is a modern tragedy. It's bad and getting worse. Unlike so many things in this challenging and uncertain world, we CAN all do something to change this. That's a rare gift...

Gentlemen!!!
Fantastic support this morning for our first ever RUOK? Day Newport Nasties event.

Some taut, trim and terrific Nasties, presented a fine spectacle for startled early risers at Bilgola Beach this morning. Impressively, 20 or so made the 6AM start. After the bastard North Face ascent out of Bilgola car park, we soon found our stride on the flat down into Newport (passing the fine figure of Boylo awaiting the L90 bus into Sydney town) and after a quick once around the surf club, flew like gazelles across the hallowed turf of Porters to Seattle's table. Curiously two props were first arrivals, raising questions about route adherence, cunning!

Matty Read (aka Seattle) was a bloody good bloke and a bloody good Nasty and a reminder to all of us for the need to get over our 'Manshit' and share when things are not going so well. It's a question of when not if, and we reflected on this over a cunningly supplied beer as we raised a glass to the one and only Seattle. Gone, but not forgotten.

The return journey was no less impressive. Wolf whistles from passing motorists almost drowned out the near-military precision of the well-honed Nasties cohort. Sadly, most of the attention was from passing tradies, but at our age, you have to take it where you can get it. Rumours have it that some telephone numbers were exchanged and a few Black Tie Ball dance cards filled.

On return to Bilgola, many took the plunge into the not-so-icy Pacific. Others commenced early engagement with local Cafe – barista of the year candidate (not) who appeared rather startled and unimpressed to be asked to make coffee before his own R&R. Suitably 'encouraged!', he rose to the occasion with the zest that only a reluctant 17 year-old can muster. We enjoyed a good chinwag – the actual point of the whole thing.

So an unqualified success gents. Another addition to the annual calendar for sure.

Mental health and suicide is a serious and growing problem. 8 Australians a day take their own lives. It IS something we can all do our bit to tackle. So let's put our hand up when we are in need (contact me or anyone else to start the conversation). Know you are all loved and that none of us are alone ..... even those with a number bigger than 8 on their backs!. In turn, we can all step up and help. RUOK? is a great start.

Bringing out the greatness in others

My favourite definition of leadership is *"the role of a leader is to bring out greatness in others"*. I was sad to learn of the recent death of George Martin. A gifted musician, producer and composer, Martin was better known to many as *'the Fifth Beatle'*. If anyone could lay claim to bringing out greatness in others, it was Sir George.

LOOKING BENEATH THE SURFACE
Pitched to him by their manager, Brian Epstein, Martin heard something he liked, even though the aspiring Beatles demo tape *"wasn't very good... in fact it was awful"*. It's now of course 'rock and roll' legend that in just a few years, he helped the four young men from Liverpool to create the greatest quantity, quality and diversity of songs in the history of music.

MORE THAN THE SUM OF THE PARTS
Martin was largely self-taught but at some ten years older than Paul, John, Ringo and George, was able to complement their raw talent by overlaying his experience of different genres, such as classical and jazz. This resulted in rich, multi-layered hits that had never been previously contemplated, let alone produced. Just think of the trumpet on *'Penny Lane'*, the harpsichord effect on *'In My Life'* or the 41 piece orchestral ending to *'A Day In The Life'*. These enhancements were not imposed, but rather suggested. Martin, never claimed to possess the genius of a Lennon or McCartney, but he did know how to help them grow. As he reflected in an interview,

> *I realised I had the ability to get the best out of people.*

The reality was Martin and the Beatles were stretching the known boundaries of sound recording almost every time they entered the studio. Martin's contribution was to guide, stretch, challenge and educate his charges. He enabled their undoubted greatness to emerge and, in the process, changed the world.

HOW CAN WE EMULATE THIS IN OUR OWN LEADERSHIP?

Chances are most of us will never possess the insight and talent of George Martin. The good news is that we don't need to in order to be great leaders. We just need to look for the talents in our people and think how we can grow and complement them. Some useful approaches are to:

Seek greatness at every level
We need to look beyond org structures and reporting lines. Talent exists in everyone and at every 'level'.

Be generous
Martin was part of extraordinary success without feeling the need to 'own it'. Be humble and celebrate the ideas and successes of the individuals and your team.

Challenge the crowd
Between 1962–1969, The Beatles produced 17 chart-topping UK singles and over 10 in the giant US market. A big part of the reason for their unparalleled success was their continuing musical evolution. They were the disrupters of their age. We too should encourage our people (and ourselves) to look for answers in unfamiliar places.

Embrace failure
A frequent theme of mine, but so vital in liberating both ourselves and our people. The experimental nature of the Martin-inspired Beatles had its share of flops. The safe route would have been to create a stream of purely derivative songs, but this was not what

happened. If we aspire to greatness we've got to get over this mental handbrake on our growth.

Have fun while you can

Teams that play together stay together – or at least do something worth doing. Nothing lasts forever and the Beatles were no different. Their split was acrimonious. The excellent Beatles Museum in Liverpool (well worth a visit) is a walking timeline of their story. The last room is very poignant. It exhibits just a white grand piano with John Lennon's picture and wire-rimmed glasses rested on it. The lyrics to *'Imagine'* adorn the wall. A sad ending, but these boys (Brian and George) had a lot of fun on the way. It's our job as leaders to make sure that our teams also make time to smile and enjoy the ride.

GREATNESS IS RELATIVE

You may not feel that your team are doing 'great' work. That does not excuse your from the responsibility to bring out their greatness. It's all relative. I spent three years leading a team of 200 people across Australia. It was a business turn around. Numbers, culture and morale were all terrible when we started. My focus was to build a leadership team and enable them to remove the barriers to their people's success. By the end, we'd transformed the numbers. The thing I am most proud of though is how many new talents we identified and grew. There's nothing more powerful and humbling than helping someone to realise their own potential and to watch their confidence and self-belief grow. It is literally life-changing.

Every day you are fortunate enough to lead a team is a gift (yes really!). You are in a position to bring out greatness in another human being. That's a rare gift. Do not squander it. You never know, like George Martin, you may be just about to start something extraordinary.

Re-thinking what winning looks like by mastering Collaboration

Collaboration is one of those bullshit bingo buzz-words that gets tossed around organisations like confetti. It implies 'teamwork' and that 'we're all in it together'. Which of course is how it should be – it's just rarely true. The reality of many businesses is that the environment is far from collaborative. Getting ahead is typically a competitive and political process. Knowledge is hoarded as a source of power and rivalries between individuals and departments are commonplace. Plus ça change you might say. Yes, but re-constructing our organisations and people to become truly collaborative is one of the key shifts we need to make to win in a VUCA world.

THE TWO FACES OF COLLABORATION
The word collaboration has two meanings. The first is to work with others on a joint project with intent to create a positive outcome. The second is more sinister – essentially to work with an enemy in a treacherous act. Whilst the second meaning has its roots in Vichy France amongst other places, its notable that our modern need to collaborate has elements of *both* meanings. Yes, we need to get better at working together within our business. But we also need to become open to partnering with other players, some of who may be former or even current competitors. Such are the demands of the disrupted world, that established businesses need to enter partnerships which even a few years ago would seem unthinkable.

SLEEPING WITH THE ENEMY
Collaboration with former competitors can be a smart play. In 2015, Tesla gifted millions of dollars worth of patent IP to its electric car competitors. It wants them to advance and share the cost of building the fuelling infrastructure necessary for electric vehicles

to reach mass viability. Sharing research, duplicated resources and other common technologies is becoming an essential evolution for many businesses. Most news organisations for example now share reporters and 'feeds'. The faster that a business can 'get over itself' to re-think collaborative possibilities, the more likely it is to prosper.

EQUIPPING OUR PEOPLE TO COLLABORATE
It's time then to give our employees the skills, mindsets and mandate to collaborate instinctively and effectively. Collaboration is one of the 4 key Competencies in the i4 Neuroleader model developed by Silvia Damiano, founder of the About My Brain Institute. (The others are *Performance, Innovation* and *Agility*). We define Collaboration as:

> *The attainment of a common goal through the effort of a combined body of people working together.*

Supported by neuroscience, the model deconstructs Collaboration into 4 constituent parts (or Pillars).

Part 3: Creating a winning mindset | 155

PERFORMANCE
- INTEGRATION
- BALANCE
- ETHICS
- MENTAL READINESS

COLLABORATION
- INSPIRATION
- COMMUNICATION
- GENEROSITY
- COURAGE

INNOVATION
- IMAGINATION
- DRIVE
- CURIOSITY
- ATTITUDE

AGILITY
- INTUITION
- AWARENESS
- INFLUENCE
- ADAPTABILITY

© SILVIA DAMIANO

The 4 pillars are: *Inspiration, Communication, Generosity* and *Courage*.

Understanding and adjusting our abilities, traits, attitudes and behaviours in each of these equips us to improve our competency to collaborate.

Inspiration
This refers to the energy, enthusiasm and desire to act as a result of feeling both mentally and emotionally stimulated. It's generated through activities, attitudes and behaviours such as:

Vision,
Passion and
Trust

In a corporate context, we need to create an environment that encourages and supports inspiration. Culture can either enable or kill inspiration. An organisation with no vision beyond short-term performance, with poor or inauthentic leadership and low levels of trust is not going to inspire its employees to go beyond the bare minimum. Crucially, inspiration, like willpower, expires. It must be re-kindled each day. Irregular 'rally the troops' motivational speeches from head office do not serve. Strategies like creating stimulating meeting spaces (check out Google and Atlassian's offices) and places (walk, go into nature), sharing hopes and taking the time to get to know co-workers can contribute to the creation of a truly inspiring workplace.

Communication
This is having a well-developed set of abilities to impart information or exchange thoughts, ideas and feelings with others. It's about both the clarity of our own thinking and expression and the ability

to actively listen to others. Key elements are:

Presence
Self-expression and
Chunking Down

Communication is at the heart of any group and any business. We've all experienced workplaces where communication is stymied, top-down, inconsistent or just absent. If ambiguity is one of the constant paradigms of our new business reality, mastering communication must be a priority. In most workplaces it needs to be re-thought. It must embrace learning from every level of the business and become attuned to emotions as well as ideas. It is the currency of the Imagination Age.

Generosity
This is about developing a kind disposition and an altruistic manner when interacting with others. It's not a word often thought of in a business context, where military or sporting metaphors of smashing the enemy or beating the competition prevail. That's a big shift. It involves adopting approaches such as:

A win-win approach
Thinking beyond self
Willingness to help

To many these may appear weak or counter-intuitive in the 'war' of business. Yet, the VUCA world means 'winning' looks different. It's a reality and the starting point is a generosity rather than scarcity mindset.

Courage
This is about our ability to face difficult circumstances despite being

fearful. It includes saying what needs to be said and the wisdom to accept what cannot be changed. Elements include:

Fear management
Ability to redirect efforts and
Trying new things

As the brilliant American psychologist Dr Brené Brown recently said in a presentation in Sydney, bravery not bravado is what makes for the best leaders.

"Are you willing to be uncomfortable?" Brown asked. *"To me that's the bottom line."*

HOW DO YOU COLLABORATE?
This is a challenging question for us all. We need to rethink what winning looks like. We may need to cede control and give voice and power to others as part of a trust-building process. That's exposing. Our own failings and fears may become apparent. If we can take that leap of faith however and encourage our colleagues to do the same, we will be able to genuinely access the collective wisdom, energy, wit and sense of fun that can make our work both more successful and enjoyable.

Worth a try?

5 things your best people will hate

You've hired some great young people to take your business to the next level. You've invested a ton of time, undergone a rigorous recruitment process and – if your sector is especially hot (like IT) – probably also paid a handsome recruiter's fee. So once they are on board, what are the best things you can do to ensure your young guns learns to hate the place?

RIDICULOUS – MAYBE NOT!
At first glance, the question is ridiculous. Why would you go through the hassle and expense of hiring great people and then do nothing to retain them? Yet, according to the 'Deloitte Milennial Survey 2016', *"Two-thirds of Millennials express a desire to leave their organization by 2020"*. So, what's the best way to go about pissing off your super talent?

1. IGNORE THEIR VALUES
Millennials are now in their mid twenties to mid thirties. Like all of us, they still like money, but they're more likely to be attracted to and invest their time in organisations that reflect their values. So if you have no clearly expressed values, or espouse one thing and do another, you're well-placed to become a recruiter's favourite customer.

2. JUST FOCUS ON THE NUMBERS
These are thoughtful souls who, in many markets, now make up the largest portion of the workforce. They are more likely to align with organisations that have a purpose beyond just profit. Banging on about the latest sales quarter and ignoring environmental or social consequences of the company footprint is the way to get them seeing red

3. PRETEND IT'S STILL 1985

Perhaps surprisingly, Millennials are rather conservative. The Deloitte report finds they *"appear to be steered by strong values at all stages of their careers; it's apparent in the employers they choose, the assignments they're willing to accept, and the decisions they make as they take on more senior-level roles"*. They also prize work/life balance (whatever that is!). If you still have a healthy '*greed is good*' dynamic in play, chances are you will be attending a lot of leaving dos.

4. LET THEM SINK OR SWIM

This group loves to keep learning and growing. They actively seek out businesses that can provide opportunities for personal development. They especially love to be mentored by both external and internal experts. 94% of those surveyed described mentoring as a positive experience (which is also a great way to create intergenerational connection). Skimping on learning and development and providing poor or unimaginative sheep-dip training is a great way to keep the on-boarding programs full.

5. PAY LIP SERVICE TO CULTURE

Investing in cultural development still appears to be viewed as a waste of time and money by many leaders. This is an excellent attitude to stick to if you want to keep staff turnover figures humming along at 20-30% plus. (Indeed I recently heard of a business with a 70% annual staff turnover!). The Deloitte survey found that 76 percent of respondents are more likely to report high levels of satisfaction where there is a creative, inclusive working culture.

THE GAME HAS CHANGED

Like it or not, we are now in the Imagination Age. The power of ideas, rather than knowledge (commoditised by Google and Co) will drive successful businesses. Ideas come from people!

Attracting and retaining the best talent is now imperative. It turns out that investing in the creation of a sustainable business that values and grows its people and interacts positively with the community and broader world is good for everyone – and the bottom line.

Finding your bravery in unexpected places

In these uncertain times it's so easy to get stuck. In a recent PWC report, media expert Megan Brownlow, expressed her pessimism about the Australian sector outlook where businesses are reducing both spend and campaign ambition.

We have to educate a raft of business leaders that behaving in the risk averse way that they are, is actually the risk.

Similarly, I recently enjoyed a fantastic keynote by 'think bigger' advocate Margie Warrell, who said;

We constantly underestimate the cost of inaction.

Whether we lead others or just ourselves, there's never been a more important time to get or keep moving. The only useful response to our VUCA world is to go forward – to challenge ourselves, to innovate, to experiment. Yet our innate human instinct to safety and our bias to risk-aversion is working against us. Cracking this mindset is a critical self-leadership skill.

LIFE IS SHORT

I was speaking with Nicki, my wife, recently and we reflected on how fickle life can be. We know this of course and yet the horrific events in Manchester and London remind us of our fragile reality. The best way we can respond positively to the heartbreaking news is to step up. As George said, "CHOOSE LIFE". We must be brave. We need to build our people, build businesses and – most importantly – build ourselves.

ALL WORK AND NO PLAY…
Getting this mix right is hard. It's important to make our mark, to build successful businesses and to make money (whilst enjoying the process). It's equally important to make and take the time to love, laugh, create and connect.

LET'S GET BRAVER
The trouble with bravery is that it's scary! I believe the key is to start small and wrestle with this sucker every day. I've recently made a bravery pact with a former client and now friend. We've agreed to hold each other accountable to regularly stepping out into discomfort to grow our businesses, our lives and our influence.

THANK YOU FOR THE MUSIC
Last weekend, Nicki and I went to see an ABBA Tribute band (I know!). We'd been apart all week and it came up last minute, so we just decided to pitch up. On arrival, we found the audience was 90% women, with the few men present looking decidedly uncomfortable. I could have sat at the back by the bar – in my comfort zone. Instead I made the conscious decision to be brave and actually asked Nicki and her mates to dance. My Dad-dancing moves are decidedly ordinary and I initially felt very self-conscious. Before long though this little act of courage was rewarded. From what started out as an S.O.S., I conquered my Waterloo and ended up as the Dancing Queen!

BITE SIZE CHUNKS
TAKE MASSIVE ACTION TODAY doesn't work for most people. Inspiration expires. We need to rewire our brains through repeated small, yet conscious acts. Over time, this helps to switch our bias – from 'no' to 'yes', from 'safety' to 'adventure', from "I can't" to "I can". It's about taking many small steps on the way to a bigger destination – our personal, financial and leadership success.

Admiral William H. McRaven headed up the US Navy Seals elite special forces. His recommendation for bravery and success? Start by making your bed everyday!

If you make your bed every morning, you will have accomplished the first task of the day. It will give you a small sense of pride and it will encourage you to do another task and another and another.

By the end of the day, that one task completed will have turned into many tasks completed. Making your bed will also reinforce the facet that little things in life matter. If you can't do the little things right, you will never do the big things right.

And, if by chance you have a miserable day, you will come home to a bed that is made – that you made – and a made bed gives you encouragement that tomorrow will be better.

Part 4: Building your expert profile

> *The two most important days in your life are the day you are born and the day you find out why!*
>
> — Mark Twain

Resilience – It's all about perspective

One of the toughest challenges in building your successful thought leadership practice is managing the tension between the extraordinary passion you have for capturing and developing your own ideas and the vital, but, for most, far less inspirational challenge of selling them!

In the early stages, this is all about building your resilience – that thick skin that gets you through the inevitable setbacks and objections. Setbacks are just part of life of course, but they will feel bigger and are more likely to derail you in the early days when your confidence, income and *'position'* in the market are all relatively low. I've been reminded of this over the last few weeks as the Hodgson tribe has endured every possible permutation of irritation and breakdown (mostly material, but almost mental!!) from broken down cars (twice), flat tyres, parking tickets, broken (new) phones, broken (new) MacBook (yes, even Apple's not perfect!), broken central heating (when it's minus plenty outside) – you get the picture.

In a perverse way though, it's been a great experience. Resilience is an essential quality for all of us who want to make a great living selling our thoughts. The finest Japanese swords were crafted by a combination of repeated heating, folding and tempering to create blades of incredible strength. Overcoming the 'slings and arrows' that outrageous fortune throws at us through a resilient attitude similarly builds great strength in us.

The key to developing a resilient attitude is (as in so many things) to be found in shifting our perspective. A *'Thought Leaders'* colleague of mine told me how she had visited Tibet and seen such appalling poverty that she felt terrible, coming as she did from a safe and privileged Australian background. She related her shame to one of the local monks. He told her that she didn't need to feel guilty because of her relative wealth, but added that she – like all of us 3% or so of the world's population fortunate enough to be living in such prosperity – did have a duty to be happy!

From that perspective, I reckon we are all doing just fine. A little dose of hardship along the way – that's just tempering us for better things ahead.

How to build a successful business around what you know (and why thought leadership is like beer!)

BEER IS BACK!
Seven years ago, a good friend of mine set up a state-of-the-art boutique brewery. It was a new concept and, for a few months, a hive of activity as men set about the serious work of brewing and bottling their own beer. The product was excellent, but, sadly, the novelty soon wore off. It was easier to grab a *'slab'* of inferior product from the local bottle shop. In the end, convenience won out over quality. The business died.

Fast-forward just a few years. Today, you can't move in Sydney for boutique pubs and micro-breweries. Good beer is back and this time I reckon it's here to stay. The market is now ready for the idea of bespoke, more expensive but better beer.

TIME TO GET SERIOUS ABOUT BUILDING YOUR INFLUENCE?
In the same way, I believe the mainstream market is now ready for thought leadership. I hear it in my conversations with self-employed consultants and corporate leaders, I see it in the new platforms created to optimise its distribution and just today, I read it in a piece in the Australian Financial Review about the need for CEOs to get serious about exercising their power to influence through social media. In short, there are a lot of folk out there looking to equip themselves for a successful professional life after corporate, or to reinvent themselves within it.

If that's you, or you're an expert looking to get paid what you're really worth, doing what you love, the following blueprint may help. It maps out what we need to do to build a sustainable practice around our expertise. Whilst it's framed mainly for the self-employed, the principles are increasingly applicable to those building their influence *within* a business. I hope it helps.

BUILDING YOUR EXPERT PRACTICE – 9 KEYS TO CAPTURING, CONNECTING AND MONETISING YOUR EXPERTISE

There's a ton of difference between being an expert and being a thought leader. You'll require entirely different levels of pro-activity, energy, persistence and flexibility. You've got to stick your neck out. You will often have to do a lot of work on your own. My model illustrates the combination of *actions*, *attitudes* and *resources* you'll need to fast-track the growth of your expert business. It describes 3 focus stages and 3 levels within each stage. Start at the bottom left and work upwards through each state.

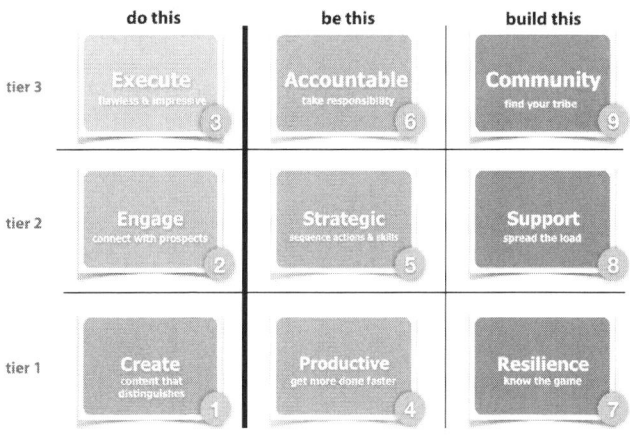

	do this	be this	build this
tier 3	Execute — flawless & impressive (3)	Accountable — take responsibility (6)	Community — find your tribe (9)
tier 2	Engage — connect with prospects (2)	Strategic — sequence actions & skills (5)	Support — spread the load (8)
tier 1	Create — content that distinguishes (1)	Productive — get more done faster (4)	Resilience — know the game (7)

mark HODGSON

1. DO THIS

Think *(capture what you know)*
The first focus stage is about what you need to *'do'*. At Thought Leaders, *'think'*, *'sell'* and *'deliver'* is a fundamental mantra. Thinking always comes first. It's about capturing what you know, understanding what problems this solves and clearly differentiating solutions.

Sell *(connect your ideas)*
Clever people often present an aversion to selling. Many subscribe to the *'build it and they will come'* mentality. In my experience they won't and don't! You've always got to be connecting your ideas with those you help and in-build this process into everything you do.

Deliver *(master flexibility)*
It's no use having amazing ideas if you can't communicate them elegantly. You have to communicate your thinking powerfully using multiple formats – workshops, videos, webinars, keynotes, 1-on-1s, blogs, tweets et al. This is the highest level skill because it amplifies both our *thinking* and our *selling*.

So that's what we *'do'*. To get real-world traction for your thought leadership, we also need to get into the right mindset to create and maintain growth. This is the focus of the second stage and is about how we need to *'be'*.

2. BE THIS

Productive *(get more done faster)*
If you are going to earn serious money for yourself or your company by selling your expertise, you have to become highly-productive (especially if you are working on your own). You need to become

ruthlessly good at getting more done more quickly and develop a constant vigilance around your output levels.

Strategic *(sequence actions and skills)*
We need to have a clear plan of where we are going. This means doing the right things at the right time. It's easy to embark on too-many projects or to get distracted. This is where 90-day horizons and strict weekly, monthly and quarterly plans are crucial. You need to schedule your activities and say *"no"*. It's about developing the discipline to finish what you've started (and avoiding shiny project syndrome).

Accountable *(take responsibility)*
Most of us can't do this alone. The best way to keep on track is to hold yourself accountable to someone else. An external mentor is the perfect person to challenge and correct us and also to encourage us to keep delivering on our agreed actions and targets.

The combination of our '*doing*' and '*being*' is a great start to developing and deploying our thinking. The final column details the things that we need to be '*building*' over time. These are fundamental in sustaining us to enjoy long-term success.

3. BUILD THIS

Resilience *(know the game)*
Business can be tough. Creating a great living selling your expertise is not easy – in fact it's the hardest thing I've ever done. It's also the most rewarding. I know it's the best way to fulfill all of my financial, energetic and legacy goals. You will experience knock-backs and discouragement – GUARANTEED. You must counter this by learning to expect and accept this fact of life and to develop your resilience muscle.

Support *(spread the load)*
To help manage your resilience, to stay on strategy and to thrive in a potentially lonely environment, it's important to build a supporting community. As you build your practice, you must actively seek out and commission those who you *'get'* you and what you are about. These are the kindred spirits, willing to support your growth.

Community *(find your tribe)*
The ambition of becoming a thought leader in your field can seem audacious, unrealistic and even arrogant. If you've got this far, you probably think you have something to offer the world. GOOD FOR YOU! You're probably right. One approach I love that breaks down this mental block is to understand that we only need to build a community over time of perhaps 10-50 clients who love what we do. We are not looking to become the next Richard Branson or Anthony Robbins. We just want to serve a small group of people who we're passionate about helping. That's all!

TRUE NORTH

I find that getting clear on the 9 parts of the Practise Plan is clarifying. It's easy to get lost and discouraged on this journey. Not only have you got to develop, sell and deliver brilliant ideas, you've got to run the whole show, often working in isolation. Keeping a lightness of touch and a good sense of humour and humility is also useful.

3 sweet spots

SWEET SPOTS – FOR YOUR GREAT IDEAS TO HIT

A recent study by *Rainmaker* – the online platform for sales and marketing professionals – showed that speaking at tradeshows and writing white papers for your market are now ranked as some of the best ways to sell any product or service. Clients trust informed people. As a result, expertise and authority have become very real business currencies. The more you are seen as an authority, the more you can charge for what you know and do. Simple.

To create this aura of authority around YOUR expertise, you need to be able to organize your ideas in way that hits 3 'sweet spots':

Clarity: Your message must be sharp and accessible to most of your audience most of the time. We all have communication bias. We may be highly visual and love diagrams, or highly auditory and love to listen. We may like detail or just want to see the bigger picture. We 'transmit' as we like to 'receive'. In other words, we are great at connecting with people just like us. Trouble is, most people aren't! In failing to adapt our delivery to this fact, we miss so much opportunity. When we learn to pitch our thinking in a way that connects with all of these learning preferences, we instantly multiply our productivity and results. It's like doubling the number of sales meetings we have just by creating clarity for more of those already in the room. The more people who 'get' you, the more will buy what you are selling.

Flexibility: Your ideas can be used repeatedly in different formats. You need to be able to quickly adapt your best thinking so that it can be used in any sales format – perhaps a sales pitch, a workshop, a speech or an article. If you spend hours extracting and re-working your thoughts from one format to another, you are wasting time and money. You need to spend more time earning, less time preparing.

***Integrity*:** Your thinking is received by your audience in a way that retains the original meaning. We've all played Chinese whispers. It's so easy for what we say to be misunderstood or lost in transition. Our best solutions need to be received with complete integrity and – ideally – be able to be passed on, in-tact, by others without us even being present. That way our solutions and influence can exist independent of us and be explained to and bought by people we've never met. This multiplies your effectiveness, builds your 'expert authority' and leverages your value.

Mastering these 3 sweet spots is a great way to get the most from any sales opportunity or audience. If you just get 20% better at each, the cumulative effect would be to increase your sales, productivity and effectiveness by over 50%.

Nothing fails like success

I recently attended Matt Church's excellent new *'Mega-Productivity'* workshop. We were looking way beyond the typical mechanical improvements (use lists, important over urgent, template everything etc etc). These are OK for creating incremental improvement, but that's no longer enough. To thrive in a world of ever-increasing competition from both mature and, increasingly, emerging challengers, most of us need to create EXPONENTIAL increases in our output. One key to these is to create entirely new mindsets.

OPEN UP
The first is that we need to be open to changing the habits of a lifetime. This is tough. We must become teachable, to question and to unlearn what has served us in the past but may not now be the best way. This single step can freshen us up and break open a whole new world of approaches.

GET UNREASONABLE
Secondly, we need to become *"blessed with dissatisfaction"*. We must be unreasonable – uncomfortable with the status quo, challenging and questioning continuously. My best boss was like this – forever pushing for more, asking for the seemingly impossible, to be achieved quicker, better and cheaper! She was tough to work for, but boy did we get some great stuff done.

A DAILY BATTLE WITH OUR WEAKER SELF!
Thirdly, we must elevate the importance of our own productivity and measure it daily. Most productivity approaches are like diets – good for a while, but hard to stick to beyond a few weeks. We fall off the wagon and back into old ways. The trick is to understand that we are not machines, that we do have good, bad and average

days. We need to create little games and constructs that keep us productive, even on days when we'd rather go to the beach, the mall or the pub!

SHOW ME THE MONEY

It's easy to view productivity as rather dull and mechanical. Getting mega-productive though is probably the biggest single factor in creating commercial success around what we know.

Going global from your bedroom!

I've had some great comments on my new blog header design (thank you). This set me to thinking about how it's actually symptomatic of quite a few principles that support the successful thought leader – whether in corporate life or as a solopreneur. Let me explain.

My new banner was designed by a Romanian freelancer I have never met. It cost 30 minutes of my time to brief and review Alina's work and an investment of $5 using fiverr.com.

Once I was happy, I sent the banner and my blog to Kathryn, my brilliant Business Manager who lives in the UK (even though I spend over half my time in Sydney, technology makes this not only possible but really simple). Kathryn then spent 1 hour emailing the blog to my list and posting onto various relevant groups and some social media sites. Cost – 30 minutes of my time and 1 hour of Kathryn's.

And so it goes…. My point is that this is just a small example of the strategies that we need to employ to maximise our productivity, impact and ultimately value as thought leaders. After 20 years of successful corporate life, I am now employing a whole new set of approaches, tools and skills to leverage what I know into the world to make a great living. I have a fraction of the resources that exist inside most businesses and yet I am confident that I am way more productive than many.

SOME HOT PRINCIPLES

1. *Think, Sell, Deliver*
   As a thought leader, your job is to THINK (develop your IP),

SELL (yes, you have to sell your thinking to clients who will value it – the missing link for many!) and DELIVER (mentor, workshop, speak your thinking for ££$$). Everything else should be done by someone else (who is more focused and skilled at e.g. editing videos, booking venues, online marketing).

2. *Leverage geo-arbitrage*

   This is much more that just outsourcing. It's the idea of accessing quality resources in less expensive parts of the world, with technology as the enabler. I've lived in Central Europe and Moscow and the educational standard in both places is very, very high. So an Alina in Romania can do for $5 what a designer in London or Sydney will charge 10 to 30 times more to do. Importantly, this is not an exploitative relationship, as talented individuals can earn many times what they can in their local economy.

3. *Opportunity and Threat*

   1st world businesses should be accessing this extraordinary global talent pool too. Myriad services exist from design to research, administration, online marketing and all manner of virtual assistants in countries like the Philippines (check out chrisducker.com for more) Organisations need to trial and integrate this into their existing bricks and mortar operations. Many businesses I know of have massive office, staff and associated costs and productivity levels at a fraction of what is now possible. There is great opportunity for those who can do this well to increase their speed and reduce costs and, of course massive risk that if they don't they will lose out to smarter competitors who get the game has changed!

4. ***Do not procrastinate on perfection***
A golden rule for all businesses large or small. It is better to get your thinking/product/idea out today 80% good than in a month at 99% good. My new banner is pretty good, but it could be better. Right now, it's a poor use of my time to spend half a day getting closer to perfection.

Successful businesses must get more comfortable with living on the imperfect, ragged edge of innovation and failure. They must become more like a collective of entrepreneurs (or employeepreneurs). This is truly thought leadership in action.

5. ***Momentum creates opportunity***
It is better to move, however imperfectly, than to endlessly ponder. Once we start to get out IP, our thinking, our solutions and opinions out into the business world, we start to get a reaction – most of it good. On the back of last week's blog I have already established some great (and completely unexpected) connections that I know will lead to fantastic commercial outcomes

So all that from a new banner!

The power of position

If you want to see Joshua Bell, one of the world's finest violinists, in concert, you can expect to pay £50–£90. You'll also typically be *'sharing him'* with several thousand other concert-goers. No surprise then that Joshua regularly commands £30,000–£50,000 for a couple of hours work.

In 2007, the *Washington Post* set up Joshua as a busking violinist in the Washington subway. He played for 45 minutes. 1,097 people passed him and, despite the fact that he is one of the world's *'gun'* violinists (and finished his set with with a towering account of one of the peaks of the solo violin repertoire – Bach's D minor Chaconne!), a grand total of 7 people stopped to listen! He earned $32 (and change).

A great story and lots of lessons for anyone looking to make a living selling their expertise in the knowledge economy. I can see three big ones;

1. *'Build it and they will come'* … NOT. Endlessly perfecting our expertise without Selling it does not work – however brilliant we are.
2. What we can charge for our expertise is entirely dependent on the context in which we are positioned. If we pitch like a busker, we'll earn like one!
3. How we are perceived is entirely in our power! (This is a big idea and one for us all to chew on!). It's largely up to us to create our expert 'position' in the market. Our choice to be seen as a hot ticket item (like Joshua in the concert spotlight) and not as a music student 'fiddling up' the night's drinking money.

At Thought Leaders, we call this building *'Position'*. As the model below shows, we need to graduate through multiple stages in building our thought leadership.

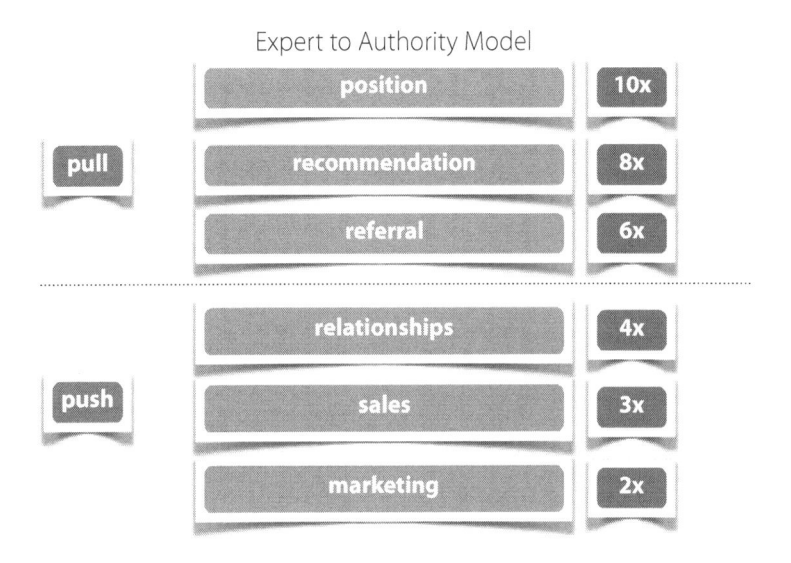

Expert to Authority Model

pull/push	Stage	Multiplier
pull	position	10x
pull	recommendation	8x
pull	referral	6x
push	relationships	4x
push	sales	3x
push	marketing	2x

At a basic level we need to actively market and sell ourselves and, of course, build relationships.

These are all essential skills and we reckon that these activities, done well, will generate 2, 3 and 4 times the level of interest compared to doing nothing to sell ourselves. In hard £ terms this could mean the difference between charging £50 and £200 an hour. Vital as these skills are, they require our constant efforts – in other words they are *'Push'* activities.

As thought leaders, we need to move beyond these. We need to create *'Pull'*. That's when what we do is so good that we become noticed and people are attracted to us. Our skill and targeted networking strategy means that influencers in our market not only start talking about us, they actively refer us – *"if you want to know about building great cultures you need to work with XXXX. I'll introduce you"*. Ultimately we become known as leading experts in our specialist field. We have *'position'* and can now command top rates for our consultancy, our keynote, our workshop, our coaching. You can probably think of a few people in your market who are in this space. These are the thought leaders.

Of course, all this assumes that you have great stuff and that what you do is clearly differentiated. That's the price of admission to the world of *'Pull'*.

Lessons learnt

I've been back in London for a year, after 17 spent overseas. 12 months after launching Thought Leaders UK, I thought it time to reflect. One thing's for sure, it's been incredibly tough. Launching Thought Leaders and brand *'me'* into a flat-lining economy with zero existing network was character building to say the least! There were more than a few *'dark nights of the soul'* and doubts aplenty. *"Is anyone out there?"*, *"Am I/is this as good as I hope/think?"*, *"Does anybody care?"*, *"Should I go back and get a job?"* ... sound familiar?

It has also been BRILLIANT. The ripples created by a mountain of activity (keynotes, blogs, meetings, presentations, workshops, webinars, whitepapers, tweets et al) are now returning.

We've reached a tipping point. The vision is becoming a reality. At Thought Leaders, 'our curriculum is our strategy' (i.e. we do what we teach!). It works – and we have already written over £40,000 of business in January.

So here, in no particular order, are my thoughts on key activities, success strategies and common pitfalls. Traps I've fallen into, mistakes I've made and, hopefully, some small gems of wisdom gained.

NETWORKING

Most organised network events I attended were a waste of time and energy, with only the organisers making money! I spent a few months learning this important truth and then moved on. I met so many smart people stuck in the networking *'timesuck'* without questioning their return or outcomes. Hope is not a strategy!

Creating a strategic approach to building a network – that's completely different. It took a while, but I've made the first 3 of the 15 or so key contacts I know I'll need to drive my business and achieve my vision. Connecting with quality contacts who *'get'* what you do and want to partner or help with introductions is pivotal. *'Connecting is not enough'* is a great *'How-to'* book on this, by my friend, Andy Lopata.

ONLINE DISCUSSIONS

Another potential time vortex! Two years ago I completed an MBA, part of which was assessed by online dialogues with fellow students. We developed multiple responses to each week's teaching. Great stuff in the academic world, sure. But many online discussions groups (e.g. LinkedIn groups) look exactly the same – full of clever people trying to impress each other with their expertise. Interesting, yes, but an effective business development strategy – probably not. It's easy to get sucked in (and I did sometimes), but consultants rarely buy from each other, so why spend hours impressing your peers? Often, it's just procrastination – a diversion from the business of actually asking others to buy our expertise.

As thought leaders we need to do just three things; *'Think', 'Sell'* and *'Deliver'*. *'Thinking'* is the piece that most experts most enjoy (and what's paraded in the discussions). *'Selling'* our ideas though, for many, the toughest part, yet it's equally important. For that reason it's also what I spend a lot of time on in our flagship *'Sell Your Thoughts'* programme.

It's better by far to demonstrate our expertise in a commercial way. I've been patiently building a distribution list and have begun to enjoy some success through it. It takes time, but it works. Many thought leaders do this really well with newsletters, blogs and white papers.

One of my favourites, Torben Rick (ace name!) distributes a great weekly blog on his thought leadership (change and disruption). It just oozes his expertise in an intelligent, accessible and elegantly commercial format. (Check out torbenrick.eu)

GET SERIOUS ABOUT YOU?

Many people who like the idea of selling their expertise are not prepared to take the vital step of investing in their development. I've invested at least £15,000 in my personal development over the last 5 years and have grown exponentially in my learning and earning as a direct result. I'm far from the finished article, but have definitely developed a more open and teachable mindset.

By contrast, I've met at least 50 smart people who told me they wanted to build their expert practice, but who will not make the leap – to financially and emotionally commit to their growth. There's never been a better time to step up and the alternative of scraping by (unfulfilled, underpaid and unhappy) is bleak. So, as Mork said, *'carpe diem!'* (See my earlier blog *'Are you serious?'*).

BUILD A GREAT SUPPORT AND ACCOUNTABILITY NETWORK

It took me a while to get this in place and to understand its profound importance. I believe the two toughest aspects of working alone are sustaining motivation and staying highly productive. If we let self-doubt dominate our thinking, or become undisciplined, both the quality and quantity of our output can nosedive. Whole days, even weeks can slip by. A destructive negative cycle can easily develop.

The solution is to build a close network of people whose input you value (and to who you are willing to be held accountable). My network is global, typically others from the Thought Leaders community. They are trusted partners, each sharing the same journey as me.

We swap experiences and hold each other accountable to deliver on our projects (e.g. make at least 15 sales calls by Friday or get out that white paper by month end). I make sure I have at least one session a week. It's often the most important 60 minutes in my diary and vital in keeping me motivated and focused. If you are not already in such a network, reach out and create one.

They are usually mutually beneficial and, in my experience, the right people will be only too willing to participate.

BACK YOUR VISION

I gave up a secure corporate career and moved my family across the world to launch Thought Leaders into the UK. I did this because I wanted to develop and commercialise my own expertise, to help others fulfill their own vision and because I am convicted that our brilliant curriculum answers so many of the questions posed by the extraordinary times in which we live.

I know so many others who have similar visions, developed or nascent, but who lack the confidence to go for it. Whilst my journey has been tough, it's now bearing fruit in so many ways (financial being just one of them). I can only encourage you to back your ideas and have a red hot go! As they say in Oz, *'don't die wondering!'*

The good, the not so good and the happy ending!

Festivities, DONE! Too much of everything as usual, but great to spend some time with my beautiful (and patient) family. I hope you also managed to find some peace and joy amongst the frenzy.

So a good time to reflect on the good and the bad of my continuing mission to create a great living doing what I love and working with people I like. Too much to ask? I don't think so. We only get one go at this life, so we should look to put in and get out the maximum, right? Hopefully some of what follows may help you to put your own year into perspective.

THE GOOD

Momentum is building nicely. From a stone cold start in 2012 when I stepped out of an organisational leadership role, across 2013 I replaced my corporate salary. Looking forward, I know about 10 times more projects and programmes than this time last year. Translation – I am looking at a full year outlook of at least $400k/£240k. It's not all about the money of course, but maintaining a commercial focus is crucial if we are not to get lost in dead ends and time-sucks. It's also important not to shy away from continuously monitoring our revenue performance. We need to place a high value on our activity and always ask the question – is what I am doing now the best use of my time?

My network of quality people is growing. I met some great new people in both the UK and Australia in 2013. It 's so important to surround ourselves with people who will feed, inspire and challenge us. The further I go on this journey, the more I believe that learning to be continuously productive is key. So consciously connect with excellent people – people who are already where you want to be. Those operating at a higher level (income, thinking, productivity…), those who will take the time to believe in you and be part of your own journey. By the same token, say goodbye to people in your world who do none of these things – the doubters, the naysayers and the cynics. You can't afford to carry passengers or anyone who saps your energy and spirit.

My productivity is much higher. Still a long way to go, but definitely getting better. When I get to hang around with some seriously talented people who are already playing the expert game brilliantly, one of the most striking things is how hard they work and how productive they are. Much of their success comes simply because they are able to produce and distribute great content very, very quickly. This is where not only fantastic tools (such as our IP snapshot), but also mindsets become so important. 80% good done in 3 hours trumps 90% good done in a week. Get it done, get it out of the door and test it in the market. Then refine. Procrastinating on perfectionism is the biggest barrier to most clever people reaching their true potential.

I put on my first Virtual Assistant – a masterstroke! Kathryn is my fantastic Business Manager. I began working with her in September and she has not only super-charged my productivity, but also helped create a great sense of team around what I am doing (see above). We've got BIG PLANS for 2014 to further leverage the partnership. In essence the arrangement means that I do what I am good at (Think, Sell, Deliver) and leave things I am less good at (lots!), or can more productively outsource to Kathryn. This is a real game changer. I very highly recommend this approach – in fact, I think it's pretty much essential to create the productivity and capacity that we need to succeed (and to prevent us procrastinating). Check out chrisducker.com to find out how you can recruit and get the best from your own VA.

I partnered with some great clients. They say that the best way to learn is to teach. I agree. This year, I worked with some fantastic people – both independent experts and employees in organisations such as Microsoft. It's so rewarding to help clever people access and connect what they know and the positive feedback is priceless. Thank you!

THE NOT SO GOOD (LET'S CALL IT WORK IN PROGRESS!)
Some of the biggest barriers to our success as self-employed experts, consultants and thought leaders are unspoken. Here are a few I wrestle with that I think are important to name. They are a vital part of the overall expert package that we need to master. For me they are a work in progress!

1. It can be very lonely pushing your own barrow.

2. The absence of positive feedback and affirmation that what you are doing is good/worthwhile/valuable can lead to doubt and plenty of it – especially if, like me, you come from a corporate background.

3. Working alone you must make literally hundreds of decisions every day – ranging from what programmes to run to how many business card to print. Big or small, this process can be exhausting. It's easy to begin to doubt our own judgement and abilities.

4. Our willpower is limited – we need to get smart around strategies to keep us on track in the absence of others holding us to account.

5. The lack of certainty (on multiple fronts) can lead to worry that flows into family life. If you want an easy ride – this ain't it!

Wrapping it all up, it's been an overwhelmingly good year. I've certainly been stretched and grown in so many ways and isn't that really the point of it all? Too many people I meet are trapped, unhappy in an un-testing and unfulfilling mediocrity. Surely we owe ourselves and the people we can help so much more don't you think?

AND FINALLY – A VERY HAPPY ENDING
I'll finish with a story that I reckon puts all of this into perspective. Last week, I had the privilege of saving someone's life.

I was looking for some friends at one of the local Sydney beaches. I missed them, but decided to go for a swim anyway. It was around 6.30 in the evening – there were a few swimmers close in and a surfer further out. The lifeguards had packed up at 6.00, so the beach was unpatrolled.

I am a volunteer lifesaver, so I have some training in the danger signs. I noticed a young boy swimming around 40 metres out at the point where the waves were breaking, wearing goggles (which is a bit unusual for experienced ocean swimmers). I wasn't sure, but something told me to keep an eye on him, although he wasn't obviously distressed. No one else was watching (including his parents!!!). Finally, I decided to go out to him – he was definitely starting to struggle and slip under *'the break'*. As I did, he cried out – HELP! I was there in 20 seconds (lookout Ian Thorpe!) and was able to keep his head above water, calm him down and get him safely back to the beach.

Although it was all over in a couple of minutes, I've thought about it a lot since. I am convinced that if I had not been there, the boy would have drowned. It wasn't a particularly dangerous surf and as people were packing up, thinking about supper and not focused on the water, this young life nearly slipped away. Thank God I was there and able to help. Any number of circumstances could have changed that. The whole episode was a timely reminder to keep perspective on what it important and how tenuous our lives can be.

Let's not waste them!

How to become an IDEAS MACHINE

One of the greatest challenges I experience in helping people to get their ideas into the world is that they don't think they have enough of them. They can come up with perhaps 3 to 5, but then run dry. This deters them from even starting to deliver on their potential as thinkers and influencers. In our new ideas economy that's a problem.

Here are some pointers guaranteed to turn even the most constipated thinker into a free-flowing ideas machine!

GIVE YOURSELF PERMISSION TO CREATE
I often find that people have developed a mental block around their ability to think, or they feel their ideas are not worth sharing. That's a natural and universal fear, but it's not true. We need to shift this by consciously giving ourselves permission to think and share.

NOT ALL IDEAS NEED TO BE BIG ONES
A second common blockage is the mis-conception that all of our ideas need to be brilliant. This is creatively paralyzing and, again, not true. There is a lot of merit in sharing even simple ideas. Where we add value is by applying them in a specific context to give them relevance for our market.

FEED YOUR BRAIN
We need to be constantly feeding our brains with new ideas. That means reading/watching/hearing and otherwise absorbing great content from a wide range of sources and disciplines. I'm constantly amazed by how poor many leaders are in this respect – with predictable results!

FRAMEWORKS HELP

We can be smart about ways we re-purpose or re-ex. same concept from different angles to create new insight by u. frameworks. There are several good ones. A favourite of mine is STEEPLE. Simply take your point and consider it from the following perspectives:

Sociological, Technological, Economic, Environmental, Political, Legal and Ethical. It's a great device to generate a multiplicity of fresh thoughts and the process itself often throws up new ideas.

BUILD ON OTHERS WORK

Not all of our ideas need to be original. A fantastic approach that Thought Leader's founder Matt Church teaches is to ask ourselves what WE think of an acknowledged thinker's ideas. We call this, Yes AND & Yes, BUT. Yes AND – is where we agree and then add our own nuance or qualification. Yes, BUT is where we may disagree – e.g. *"XYZ was right to say ABC in 2010, BUT the growth of 123 in 789 means that everything has changed"*. This process both acknowledges the value of the original ideas and positions us as informed thinkers by developing them to be relevant in a specific time, industry or geography. In other words, it makes us look smart).

In an ideas economy, ideas are the new business currency. Building your ideas bank is a necessity. The ability to consistently connect your thinking with the market you serve creates a hard-to-replicate competitive edge. As shown here, I believe it's well within the grasp of anyone willing to invest the time and take a chance.

Getting stuff done in a world of one!

I'm livid. I've just sent the final cover design for my new book, 'Time to Shine – adjusting who you are and what you know to succeed in the ideas economy' to the printers. In less than a week, I'll have the first copy in my hot little hand – ready to be sent to a long list of current and potential customers. The reason I'm annoyed is that I could have done this months ago. I wrote the book in March but then allowed the few small final steps (proof, cover design, introduction, etc) to delay the entire project. Why – because I don't like detail. It frustrates me and I blow it up in my head to be a much bigger deal than it really is. Like my tax return, once I finally knuckled down, it was all pathetically easy. Pretty dumb for someone who makes a living helping others to unleash their expertise eh?

GETTING PRODUCTIVE IN A TEAM OF ONE
Back in my corporate days, this wasn't a problem. I had a team around me and it was easy to find people who loved the bits I didn't. When we work for us, that all changes. We've got two key challenges.

1. *Getting stuff done that we don't do well*
   This starts with self-awareness. What are you bad at? It's worth drawing up a list of key tasks and asking if you are the best person for the job. In our wired world there's not much that we can't outsource – and often for remarkably little cost. Just check out fiverr.com.

2. *Not spending time on things we may like, but are a dumb use of our time.*

This one is tougher. To run a successful thought leader practice, we've got to be ruthless about where we invest our time. A guiding mantra I like is to 'only do what only you can do'. So no hiding in administration when we should be creating IP or calling potential clients.

SHARE THE LOAD

This is where investing in an assistant is vital. I have Kathryn, my brilliant virtual Business Manager. With this blog for example I write it because only I can do that. Once created though, I send it to Kathryn who tidies it up, tags it, sends it to our email list and posts into LinkedIn and other social media. She's much better and faster at this and the task division allows me to spend my time on higher value activities that only I can do. Investing in an assistant is an essential performance upgrade that many resist for too long – stuck in the poverty mindset of bootstrapping and DIY. It's a very real tension, but the advent of well-trained and lower-cost VAs located in countries like the Phillipines now makes this much more affordable and less scary.

MASTERING ALL THIS IS A CONSTANT WRESTLE

Working for other people is easy because we get told what to do. If we don't do the right thing, we'll soon know about it. When we are our own boss, it's much harder. We are not robots and functioning with a 'carpe deum' mindset is not always our reality. We all have bad hair days when it's easy to get distracted, disheartened and wonder if we're doing the right thing. Systems and process help to a great extent, but at times we just have to ease up. Creating the life you want by selling your expertise to people you like is very possible – but it ain't easy) I'm giving myself a written warning for procrastinating on 'Time to Shine'. Next time things will be different.......

Why we're all entrepreneurs now

For the last year I've been writing two blogs. ***Pinch of Thought*** – for people who work for themselves as information experts and consultants; ***Leading Change*** – for leaders in businesses and larger organizations. My thinking was that these are two separate groups that need to be served in different ways. I've come to realize that I was wrong. Whether we work for 'Me Inc' or some version of 'Big Co, we're all the same – or we need to be. You see, we all now need to be entrepreneurs.

ENTREPRENEURS AIN'T WHAT THEY USED TO BE

Well at least not all of them. The word entrepreneur typically conjures up images of impatient, and driven young men and women who grab an idea and work feverishly to turn it into fast-growth business that they'll flip for a hefty profit. They work hard and fail often.

For many of us that sounds too high-risk and frenetic. Trouble is, the skills, agility, drive and speed of the entrepreneur are increasingly demanded of all of us. Here's why.

Job security is a myth

It's now anticipated that new entrants to today's job market will have as many as 5 careers and 20 employers. That may not be a worry for Gen Y's digital natives, but for experienced workers, managers and leaders aged 40+ who have grown up expecting job-for-life security in one or two career areas, this can be terrifying. With many jobs destined to be automated or performed more cheaply by leaner, keener workers in lower-cost markets, this is an accelerating trend.

Time-served no longer counts
Brilliant leadership thinker, Silvia Damiano argues that we have left the *Knowledge Age* and entered the *Imagination Age*. Power now comes more from ideas and the ability to implement them than through the accumulation of knowledge. That's a massive shift. No one cares if you've been in a company for twenty years if, like so many, you've stopped learning and growing.

These trends combined mean that we are now more likely to be exposed to (global) market pressures to 'perform' to secure our ongoing financial security.

Our personal and professional lives are inextricably intertwined
Technology and the increased pressure to do more with less means that we are 'always on'. Not a good thing, but the genie is out! The ability to access our work anywhere, 24/7 requires us to develop new disciplines and productivity skills if we are not to succumb to burn out and damage to our mental health and relationships. Mental health issues are a significant and growing problem for both the individual and the economy (estimated to cost over $20 billion p.a. in Australia in 2015).

We must self-lead
Both within and without formal organizations, we are expected to act more autonomously as formal accountability structures are flattened. That's another two-edged sword. With autonomy comes responsibility and accountability. Self-awareness, self-motivation and self-leadership skills become paramount.

Exciting/Scary – it depends
In this *Imagination Age,* we are both exposed and enabled. These pressures can be exciting on a good day and scary on a bad one. Managing that tension, getting and staying productive become

new skills for us to master.

WHAT MUST WE DO?

There is no sugar coating the tough stuff in this. It particularly impacts the 40-55 year olds who have been brought up in a *Knowledge Economy* with very different expectations. The rules have changed. We not only have to learn new skills, mindsets and approaches, we have to UNlearn the old ones.

At a time when we were hoping to slow down, we have to step up, to re-orientate and to re-educate. We have to learn to take risks, to embrace new technologies and to perhaps develop a blended portfolio of roles working for others and ourselves..

That's why I've decided to discontinue **Leading Change**. From now on, I'll be sending **Pinch of Thought** to all my subscribers. I'll be exploring the issues that we all face in adjusting to and thriving in this new age of ideas.

Remember, we're all in this together. None of us knows the answers and – if we're honest – we all have both our scared and (hopefully) excited days!

I hope you stick along for the ride.

Are you serious about your future success?

As I build my consultancy helping experts to become confident and successful influencers and leaders, I'm struck by how many time wasters I meet.

Of course, these people are an irritation to me. But they're also wasting their own time, resources and personal 'energy' as they flit from one free meeting, seminar or webinar to the next – picking up crumbs, but with no focus or strategy. These are not serious people. I doubt that many of them ever achieve the success they claim to seek.

SKIN IN THE GAME?

Serious people understand that they need to invest in their growth and learning. They need to acquire new skills and, patiently but surely, build the influence and positioning that's essential to achieving success in our volatile world. Serious people get that they need to have some 'skin in the game' (probably money) to help them to focus and commit.

FREE BUT NOT CHEAP

Few of us are good at valuing information, teaching or advice that we haven't paid for. Significant growth requires hard work, sacrifice and discomfort. In my experience of mentoring over 100 consultants, execs and entrepreneurs over the last few years – there are always points of disturbance and emotional growth that are tough to negotiate. They are also essential to getting great results.

If we've just rocked up for some free stuff that then asks us to commit to any of the above, we find it easy to slip, procrastinate and make excuses – after all it's cost us nothing right?

But in another sense this approach costs us everything. It robs us of our ability to actually attain what we seek. If a low risk, low-cost approach never actually delivers, isn't it just death by a thousand cuts? If you speak to those who have achieved the success you want, you'll find pretty much all of them have invested (often significantly) in their growth.

If you aren't serious about you, why should anybody else be?

Part 5: Mastering communication

I've learned that people will forget what you said, people will forget what you did, but people will never forget how you made them feel.

— Maya Angelou

What's wrong with you?

For the last few weeks I've been nursing a very sore shoulder. Apparently it's a torn rotator cuff (torn I might add in act of folly involving a small rubber boat and big wet wave). All I know is it hurts (and *'man pain'* too!). Moreover, because it's my right shoulder and I am right-sided it's really incapacitating. It's been chastening to learn just how much of a bias I've developed over a lifetime – from opening a car door to putting on a coat, I've relied on one arm to do all the work. Now I am asking my left side to step us as it were.

WE ARE ALL BIASED
Most of us of course have similar predispositions. Generally we are aware of them – at least the physical ones. Far less obvious are the biases in the way we communicate and yet they can be every bit as limiting. Becoming aware of these and then consciously compensating for them is a great way for us to increase our personal and commercial effectiveness.

THINK IN FULL-SPECTRUM
This thinking is at the heart of the *Thought Leaders* IP Snapshot tool. Created by founder Matt Church, it's a great framework that maximizes our chances of being understood by most people – whatever their preference or bias. We call this full-spectrum thinking.

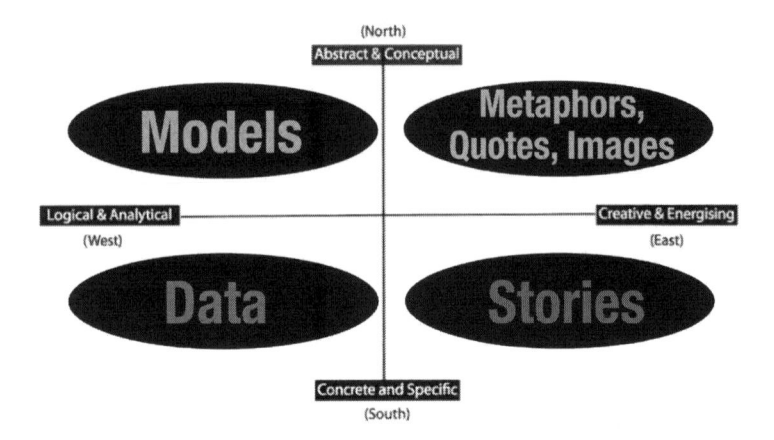

It's useful to think of our ideas as having 4 quadrants (as in the model above). Our *'point'* sits in the middle. We then make sure we illustrate it in each of the 4 quadrants (and not just the 1 or 2 we favour).

BIG PICTURE, LEFT-BRAIN
We need to express our ideas at a high level to provide context and meaning. The left-brain is about logic. Models are a great way to capture a big idea in a clear and analytical way.

BIG PICTURE, RIGHT-BRAIN
Our right brain is about emotion and creativity. Metaphors and quotes help us to embed understanding.

SPECIFIC DETAIL, LEFT-BRAIN
Most of us cover off this quadrant really well. It's the way we have been educated to think and work. This is about logic, data and detail.

SPECIFIC DETAIL, RIGHT BRAIN
We need to also express detail in a way that engages us emotionally. Stories are brilliant for this (and why businesses are belatedly

understanding the importance of using stories and narrative to engage and inspire both customers and employees)

WHERE TO START?

There is a lot of depth to this idea. Mastering this approach equips you to transform the way you connect with people. To start, you simply need to work out where your natural preferences lie. By default, you'll also identify your weaknesses. You need to concentrate on addressing these when you write, speak or present. Don't worry about your strong areas – as these are ingrained biases, you'll cover them off naturally.

Don't like stories, start telling some (Mr Google can help here!). Stuck in detail and a little dry – add a quote or a metaphor. You'll be amazed by how suddenly more people in the room seem to be *'getting'* what you are saying. You'll become an ambidextrous, two-footed, 5 ball juggling marvel!

Are you a Donkey or an Owl?

A few years ago, I enjoyed a short family holiday in Devon in the south west of England. On one *'rain day'* excursion (there were a few!!!!) we visited the *'world famous'* Totnes Rare Breeds Farm. It's home to a fascinating menagerie of creatures ranging from exotic Siberian owls to everyday goats and hens. At the mundane end of spectrum, we came across two beasts of burden – one called the *'Standard Donkey'*, the second the *'Mediterranean Miniature Donkey'*. This made me smile – two pretty much identical animals, but one so much more interesting than the other. Which donkey would you rather be at a party?

LANGUAGE IS A POWERFUL TOOL

You see, language is such a powerful tool, and one that as thought leaders and influencers we need to understand and harness. Here are a few ideas of how we can use words and language to think and connect more effectively;

1. CREATE DEPTH AND INTEREST

Varying our use of words creates a sense of richness and hierarchy. We call this linguistic palette. Red, Crimson and Vermillion all mean the same thing, but Crimson feels richer than plain old Red and Vermillion adds an extra layer of elegance and sophistication. They therefore work at different levels of abstraction and enable us to add nuance and subtlety to our communication.

2. REINFORCE THROUGH REPETITION (IN A GOOD WAY)

I am a failed naval pilot – a wannabe Tom Cruise, minus the teeth, money and need to work with short actresses! In my (admittedly short) time in the military, I was exposed the powerpoint-by-numbers rule book:

"Tell them what you are going to tell them."
"Tell them."
"Tell them what you've told them."

So imagine yourself in a cold, sterile classroom, probably at 6 o'clock in the morning...

Slide 1. *"Next we are going to talk about the importance of closing the hatch before diving the submarine."*
Slide 2. *"When diving the submarine it is important to close the hatch to avoid filling up with water and sinking forever!"*
Slide 3. *"In summary then, to avoid your mum getting an upsetting letter from the Admiral, it's important to close the hatch before you dive, dive, dive!"*

In other words, we need to repeat our message several times to get it across. Whilst research and life experience tells us this is true, there are much less crude and more effective ways;

1. **Use different words that mean the same thing** (red, crimson, vermillion).

2. **Use different types of speech** – for example *'formal'* and *'casual'*.

Formal Palette: Practice Detachment.
As you become more skilled at managing the process of a presentation, you focus less on yourself, the audience and your content and more on the whole process.

Casual Palette: Forget about you!
The better you get, the more you notice what's happening rather than what you or they are doing. It's like an out-of-body experience!

Here, we are again saying the same thing in a different way and also allowing a bit of informality and even humour. It's a great way of relaxing the meeting or presentation so that it can assume a more human, authentic and ultimately productive tone. It's a bit like getting permission to take off our jacket and loosen our tie.

3. USE WORDS TO NAME THE HIGHER CONTEXT

Higher order words can set the context for our thinking and help point to solutions. As influencers we need to constantly help our customers and audience to understand the bigger picture – to ask and answer the question, *'what is really going on?'*

Many people default to thinking in detail. When they tell us about their problems, they are often describing detailed symptoms that have been created by higher order issues that they can't see. For example, stress, absenteeism and low productivity may be less about workplace conditions and processes and more about change fear or fatigue. So *'Change'* is the real problem and the solution may be *'Authentic Leadership'*.

As we seek to lead and influence our markets, we must be the leaders in identifying larger trends and how they can be avoided or exploited. Expertly using higher order words to think and explain to others is a fantastic skill to hone.

The magic of storytelling – a speech, a poem and a song

I've just returned from a father and sons' rugby tour to Fiji. It's an annual event run for the under 14 teams at the local club where my son and I play (one rather more energetically than the other!). Over a year in the making, we work hard to create a week away that's a wonderful blend of rugby, community service and father/son *'bonding'*. We had a blast. We made new friends and had our eyes opened to just how much we take for granted in our privileged first world lifestyles.

It was a week of challenge and physicality for the boys taking on the formidable Fijian teams, but also a time for reflection. As fathers, we took time out to encourage and stretch the thinking of these young men. Of course, as part of a large tour, there was a mass of daily communication around logistics, team talks and briefings. Some of the most powerful moments of connection for both fathers and sons though came when we told stories. Here are three examples – a speech, a poem and a song – each a testimony to the mesmeric ability of story telling to stir, excite and move us.

THE SPEECH
It was the night before the *'Bula Cup'* big game day at the end of the tour. A lot of the lads were understandably nervous, so a few dads got together to perform the famous speech delivered by Henry V to encourage his over-matched army on the eve of the battle of Agincourt. (We actually performed a customised version). For the first time in a week, 60 teenage boys were transfixed by the beauty and force of the Bard. They didn't all understand the verse, but they definitely appreciated the dramatic delivery!

From this day to the ending of the world, But we in it shall be remembered. We few, we happy few, we band of brothers; For he to-day that sheds his blood with me Shall be my brother; be he ne'er so vile, This day shall gentle his condition; And gentlemen in England now-a-bed Shall think themselves accurs'd they were not here, And hold their manhoods cheap whiles any speaks That fought with us upon Saint Crispin's day.

HENRY V – William Shakespeare

THE POEM

This was impressively recited in its 13 verse entirety, by one of the dad's – prompted by a conversation about the coming-of-age hero of the iconic Australian poem. The un-named hero is 'a stripling' – probably similar in age to the boys on tour. Here's a short extract (but the whole poem is a rewarding read).

There was movement at the station, for the word had passed around
That the colt from old Regret had got away,
And had joined the wild bush horses — he was worth a thousand pound,
So all the cracks had gathered to the fray.
All the tried and noted riders from the stations near and far
Had mustered at the homestead overnight,
For the bushmen love hard riding where the wild bush horses are,
And the stock-horse snuffs the battle with delight
And one was there, a stripling on a small and weedy beast,
He was something like a racehorse undersized,
With a touch of Timor pony — three parts thoroughbred at least —
And such as are by mountain horsemen prized.
He was hard and tough and wiry — just the sort that won't say die
There was courage in his quick impatient tread;
And he bore the badge of gameness in his bright and fiery eye,
And the proud and lofty carriage of his head

But still so slight and weedy, one would doubt his power to stay
And the old man said, 'That horse will never do
'For a long and tiring gallop — lad, you'd better stop away,
'Those hills are far too rough for such as you.'
So he waited sad and wistful — only Clancy stood his friend —
'I think we ought to let him come,' he said;
'I warrant he'll be with us when he's wanted at the end,
'For both his horse and he are mountain bred.'

THE MAN FROM SNOWY RIVER – Banjo Paterson

THE SONG

We were fortunate to have several very talented musicians on the tour. There's something deeply moving about sitting down in a group and sharing a song. We sung (to varying degrees of harmony!) many, but one that stuck in my mind is the soulful story of the sinking of the steel ship, the Edmund Fitzgerald on Lake Superior. Here's a short excerpt:

The legend lives on from the Chippewa on down
Of the big lake they call Gitche Gumee
The lake, it is said, never gives up her dead
When the skies of November turn gloomy
With a load of iron ore twenty-six thousand tons more
Than the Edmund Fitzgerald weighed empty
That good ship and true was a bone to be chewed
When the gales of November came early
The ship was the pride of the American side
Coming back from some mill in Wisconsin
As the big freighters go, it was bigger than most
With a crew and good captain well seasoned
Concluding some terms with a couple of steel firms
When they left fully loaded for Cleveland

Then later that night when the ship's bell rang
Could it be the north wind they'd been feelin'?
The wind in the wires made a tattle-tale sound
When the wave broke over the railing
And every man knew, as the captain did too
'Twas the witch of November come stealin'
The dawn came late and the breakfast had to wait
When the gales of November came slashin'
When afternoon came it was freezing rain
In the face of a hurricane west wind

THE WRECK OF THE EDMUND FITZGERALD – Gordon Lightfoot

STORIES ROCK!

Three stories, each told in very different ways, but every one a great reminder of this universal truth. Stories are a great way to connect and to communicate elaborate detail to our right brain – the part that influences our creativity and emotions. This is why we deliberately include stories as an essential part of our *Thought Leaders* IP *'snapshot'* tool. We all love stories, yet few of us use them in our business communications.

Welcome to Planet Sea

There are key moments in life when we know one chapter is closing and a new one beginning. Last week, I experienced a Big One – accompanying my daughter, Izabell, to her first University open day. It seems like only yesterday that I held the hand of a very small, 4 year old girl (wearing glasses and a big hat) and walked her to her first day at primary school. Fast-forward 14 years and I'm escorting a beautiful, confident young women about to cross the threshold into adult life. Izzi plans to study marine biology and, at the open day, a tutor gave a brilliant introduction to the importance of the subject by asking one simple question. *"Why do we call our planet 'Earth' when over 70 per cent of it is covered in water?"* A great, thought-provoking observation created by simply shifting our perspective.

I noticed a similar shift in a recent newspaper article by The Times columnist, Melanie Reid. She observed the deep irony that in the same week as Scottish people are voting to metaphorically *'leave'* the UK, the numbers of illegal immigrants trying to stowaway on UK-bound trucks in France has reached epidemic proportions. As desperate thousands seek to enter the *'promised land'* by any means, millions may decide they don't want what anything that the UK has to offer. Again, it's all about perspective.

PERSPECTIVE IS POWERFUL
Shifting perspective is a smart way for us to add value to our thinking. If we are looking to influence, inform or otherwise engage others, we need to stand out. What we say must be different to the prevailing conversation. Here are some ways we can do this:

1. *Zoom out*

   Step back to create a bigger, more meaningful view. Imagine *'zooming out'* on Google Earth to see what's really going on outside of what we can see *'on the ground'*. Planet Sea is a good example.

2. *Think globally*

   Look at what's going on in other parts of the world in your industry. Who's doing well? How? Why? For example, what is Air New Zealand doing that it can announce record profits in the same week that trans-Tasman neighbour Qantas writes off its biggest ever loss?

3. *Use multiple angles*

   It's useful to interrogate an idea from different directions to unlock new insight. There are many frameworks. STEEPLE is a favourite. Easy to use, all we need to do is to ask the question, what does this idea look like viewed from each of these filters:

   S – Sociological, **T** – Technological, **E** – Economic, **E** – Environmental, **P** – Political, **L** – Legal, **E** – Ethical

Using one or several of these approaches is a great way to elevate the quality and elegance of our thinking. By coming at ideas in unexpected ways, we can also generate *'eureka'* moments for others. Mastering this is actually quite simple. Like a photographer looking for that special picture, we just need to remember to look at the familiar in unexpected ways.

Are you talking to me?

It's school holidays in Australia and my 14 year-old son is away with a couple of his mates up the coast. The mercury in Sydney has hit an insane 33 degrees (in early Spring!) Day two, it's time to check in.

SEEK FIRST TO UNDERSTAND...
What I WANT to say is – *"How are you son? I hope you are enjoying your time away, behaving well and being polite, especially to your friend's parents. Washing would be a good thing to do at some point! We love and miss you."* What I actually say – conscious of a need to try and relate is:

"Hi dude. How's it going? Hope you are having heaps of fun. Love D"

(Of course, I don't actually *'say'* anything – 14 years old boys don't talk, they only grunt and text – remorselessly. Texting is the way to go.)

The response:

"Cheers yeah it's hell good weather sick"

Thrilled, I respond:

"That's great mate, Glad you're enjoying yourself. D x"

Not sure that the kiss will be appreciated, but it kind of slipped out! I get back:

"Thanks cuz"

Now I don't know when I became *'cuz'*, rather than father or dad, but I don't mind. I just love that number one son is A. alive! and B. clearly having a great time.

We are COMMUNICATING.

WE NEED TO THINK – AND ADAPT
This is a good example of how we need to adapt what we *'say'* to connect with our audience. Too much business communication is still stuck in ritual – the metaphorical equivalent of *'telephone voice'*. We need to think – what's the right tone? Too formal and we come across as stuffy and dated (think lawyers), too casual and we appear disrespectful (think inappropriately *'matey'* call centre operator attempting to *'smile and dial'* their way into your wallet).

You'll know the right tone when you hit it. The starting point is to ask the question in the first place – *"What's the best way to say this"* – Dude!

Learning to listen

Warning. This Pinch of Thought blog is a little different from usual as I discuss suicide. If that's something about which you are sensitive for any number of valid reasons, you may want to give this one a miss. Thanks, Mark

I've just graduated from a training program and am now a very proud (and very probationary) Crisis Support Worker for Lifeline. Lifeline is a fantastic organization, best known for the telephone support service that if offers for Australians in crisis. There are plenty of us! In the last 12 months, Lifeline call support workers have answered over 1 million calls from people who are suicidal, depressed, victims of domestic abuse, suffering mental health issues or are simply lonely. That's a staggering number by itself and perhaps more tellingly, one that has increased by 25% in just a year. Whilst part of that is hopefully due to a positive increase in awareness of the Lifeline service, there's no masking the fact that more and more of us are in crisis.

GIVING TO GET

I volunteered to become a Lifeline CSW from an altruistic point of view. Like hundreds of other amazing people drawn from all walks of life, I'll be spending 8 – 12 hours a month on the listening end of the 13 11 14 national crisis support number. What has really surprised me is how much I have learned that I think will make me better at what I do as a mentor, speaker and influencer and also as a father, husband and son. Here are some thoughts that I share as they may also help you.

WE ARE ALL ON THE SAME ROAD

As a mentor, I spend a lot of time helping people go from good to really good to great. But that line goes the other way too. From good, to no-so-good, to pretty bad, to really bad, to bleakly hopeless. We are all on that line. Any one of us – irrespective of social standing, friendships, money and resources – can find ourselves at the 'low' end. That's worth remembering in our workplaces and relationships both when we are in a bad place AND when we are lucky enough to not be.

There but for the grace of God (the universe or any other belief system you hold dear) goes all of us!

DIRECT QUESTIONS ARE POWERFUL
First and foremost, Lifeline is about suicide prevention. The key thing in suicide prevention is to ask the suicide question – clearly and unambiguously. "Are you thinking about committing suicide?" "Are you considering taking your own life?"….. Many suicidal callers find the clarity of the question enables them to finally talk about the way they feel. That release can – hopefully – start the process that leads to a more positive mindset and outcome. Without being trite, we can learn from this in our other interactions. We so often skirt around issues rather than ask the direct question – be it in a business or personal context. It's not about being rude or bullying, just direct and effective. Clarity is invaluable in helping us to move forward in every context.

FIND A MIDDLE WAY TO UNFREEZE GRIDLOCK
One of the best things I learned was from a suicide prevention program called ASIST. When people are ready to take their own lives, waxing lyrically about "just choose life", or "you've got so much to live for" does not work. It's too big a leap for someone for whom suicide is a logical, preferable or inevitable step. The approach is to negotiate and introduce a third way – to agree to work together on a plan to keep the caller 'safe for now'. Even if safe for now is just an hour or

a day, we are moving them away from the immediate act of suicide. Again, without at all meaning to trivialize the seriousness of this, I think we can learn and apply the principle. It's so easy for us to get caught in unhelpful 'positions'. If we instead agree a small step in a positive direction, we may just start to establish a little momentum that can break the gridlock.

LISTEN – A LOT!
At our graduation, each newly minted Crisis Support Worker was given a large seashell – like the ones we hold to our ears to 'hear the sea'. It is a symbol that we need to listen – at least 70 per cent of the time. As someone who spends a lot of time transmitting, this was the biggest lesson (and challenge) for me. I've already spent some time on the phones with 'help seekers' and for so many of them, the most precious part of the interaction is that they feel they have been heard. In a world full of noise and superficiality, that's a gift that we can give to everyone and one that benefits us all.

Press SEND – why productivity trumps perfection when you are creating content

Writing my *Pinch of Thought* blog is something I really enjoy. The trouble is that finding the time is not always easy. When I am flat out travelling, speaking, training or mentoring, it's often the last thing I feel like doing. Sometimes it's just a royal pain in the bum. Given that no one will haul me over the coals if I don't create some more 'content gold', it's tempting to not bother. Whilst I can't claim I have never slipped (I'm only human))) I can say it's rare. You see I know just how important blogging is to my business.

MOST PEOPLE GET THIS WRONG

If you are regularly creating blogs, articles, white papers and other thought pieces give yourself a pat on the back. For the other 90+% of readers, chances are you need to get serious. That's right, studies suggest that less than 10% (and possibly as few as 1%) of professionals actually play this game consistently well. As I've written previously there are a ton of reasons why blogging is commercially smart. It's my conviction that it's no longer a 'nice-to-do' but a business necessity. The crazy thing is that it's not that hard once you get started.

WE FIXATE ON THE WRONG THING

Like so many things in life, the fear of the task is often greater than the reality. The biggest mistake is that we fixate on the wrong thing. When writing we aim for *perfection*. What we should be aiming for is *productivity*. To get started, we need to value quantity over quality. That may sound counter-intuitive. What's the point of creating blogs and other content if they're not that good? Reality though is that we will only develop the content creation muscle we need through repetition. Developing the discipline to write a blog each week (or at least fortnight) spending a maximum of 60-90 minutes is the key metric. Once we do that two things happen.

We start to create influence. Remember, if most of our competitors are not blogging about what's going on in the market and we are – consistently – we can't fail but to begin to build a reputation that attracts the connections we seek. We're creating content as a commercial activity, not to win a writing award. We are already succeeding.

We start to get good! Removing the perfectionist angst, and publishing regularly will improve the quality of what we write. I call this 'finding your voice'. Practice does indeed make perfect.

THREE IDEAS TO GET YOU OVER THE CONTENT-CREATION HUMP

Get detached
We have to become detached from the result of our creative endeavours. We need to let *'that's good enough to go'* sit comfortably. In a VUCA world, no one can afford the indulgence of perfectionism. Write your blog. Press SEND. Move on.

Imagine no one is reading
This is a good mind-trick. In a world moving at a million miles per second, our blog, however brilliant or average is unlikely to make much of a 'dent in the universe'. Chances are few people will actually read it, so it's not that important if it's less than brilliant. Switch that around and you can see that it's actually a really poor investment of your time to expend too much effort.

Understand that we're often the worst judge of what our audience likes!
I'm still constantly surprised by which blogs get the best response.

Often it's the ones that I think are a little light-on, whilst I can point to several that I thought were really special that landed like the proverbial tree in a forest … You never know, so it doesn't matter.

So have a go. No one's reading and just starting puts you in the top 10% in your field!

Why selling is now everyone's business

At the heart of the Thought Leaders methodology is a guiding mantra. We call it Think, Sell, Deliver. To maximise earnings and growth, time should be split equally between the three focus areas.

1. ***Think*** *(capture what we know)*
   Thinking comes first. It's about capturing what we know and do, understanding what problems this solves and clearly differentiating the solutions we provide.

2. ***Sell*** *(connect our ideas)*
   We have to continually connect our ideas with the clients we help. This process must live in everything we do. Too many avoid this conversation – they fail to connect their thinking commercially.

3. ***Deliver*** *(master flexibility)*
   We have to connect our ideas using multiple formats and media to meet the customer where they hang out and in the way they want.

NO LONGER A SMALL PLAYER PLAY

For a long time, we primarily used this IP to help individual consultants to differentiate themselves from other experts. It was a small business play. This has changed. Larger businesses increasingly need to think and act like a collective of internal entrepreneurs – flexible, adaptable, fast and hungry. Applying, a *Think, Sell, Deliver* focus is now an imperative. The corporate game has changed in so many ways. The sales shift is one of the most profound and least understood. Specifically, the responsibility for revenue and new business can no longer rest with a small, discrete group – a sales team or a business development unit. As Dan Pink writes in his excellent book, *'To Sell is Human'*:

> *A world of flat organizations and tumultuous business conditions punishes fixed skills and prizes elastic ones. What an individual does day to day now must stretch across functional boundaries.*

PROBLEM NUMBER 1. NO ONE LIKES SALES

Does Pink's ideal sound like your business? My guess is not. Most remain structured around traditional functions (operations, finance, marketing, customer service, sales…) – in other words, Pink's *'fixed skills'*. Typically, few people are keen to have the accountabilities of sales added to their existing remits. In fact, most corporate folk get as far away from sales as possible!

PROBLEM 2. TRADITIONAL SALES DON'T WORK ANY MORE

In the unlikely event that you do have a business chock-full of wannabe sales guns just waiting for the call, you've got a second problem. Sales have changed. Traditional sales and marketing *'push'* strategies are failing. Starved of time and overwhelmed with information, your customers are switching off to unsolicited approaches. Not only must more people in your business now sell, they need to learn new ways to do it.

THE GOOD NEWS!

For those businesses prepared to think differently, there is a solution – and it's a good one. Successful companies can now build a 'pull' strategy that attracts their target customers and partners. The best way to do this is to leverage the expertise of a whole cross-section of your staff to create the information and opinion that will help your clients to solve their problems. You can then connect this to your customer base though networks, meetings, blog posts, white papers, conference speeches, trade-articles and other touch points. It's effectively selling the skills, know-how, ideas and passion of your people. In a flat world this is all you really have to differentiate you from the rest. This is what C21 sales looks like. It's 'pull', not 'push'. The best thing is that, done well, it's something that anyone in your business can do and LEARN TO ENJOY! Mastering this approach builds a clear point of difference for your business and is a smart commercial and cultural strategy.

Leading change starts with understanding people

THE KING IS DEAD…

The overthrow of Prime Minister Tony Abbot was beautiful to behold. Deliciously timed to coincide with a lazy Monday evening's peak time TV, the events played out like a soap opera of the rich and famous. ***House of Cards – live and uncut***. Traditional Tony usurped by Modernist Malcolm. The King is dead, long live the King.

This was transformation in action and fittingly, the new Australian PM espouses the language of change.

> *We have to work more agilely, more innovatively, we have to be more nimble in the way we seize the enormous opportunities presented to us. We're not seeking to proof ourselves against the future. We are seeking to embrace it.*

Whatever your politics, this is stirring stuff. I also think it's absolutely right. We've got to get serious about leading change in our businesses. Like it or not, the future's already here. We need to equip our people to become *'agile, innovative and nimble"*. We must create the cultures, skills and attitudes that will genuinely equip our businesses to embrace and prosper from change.

IT ALL STARTS WITH THE INDIVIDUAL

There are many change approaches and programs. The best ones understand that success ultimately depends on getting people to buy-in. It's about understanding people.

Here are 5 things that may help.

1. *Inspiration Expires*
   We've got to do so much more than the rah rah! The *'once more unto the breach dear friends'* inspirational launch speech is great, but it's not enough. We have to support our change strategies with ongoing stimulation and communication.

2. *Communicate What's In It For Them?*
   The benefits of a major change may be obvious to you the leader. A bonus, perhaps shares, or an early promotion. Is that the case for your people? If not, make it clear in terms that they will care about – job security, new opportunities, better conditions. Plan benefits beyond the commercial – e.g. convert a percentage of a productivity gain into a 'causes pool'. Most staff are unlikely to get too excited by a 7% increase in XYZ productivity, but they will love to feel that their actions enable them to contribute to something that IS important such as a community charity.

3. *Get OK with Failure*
   Change is inherently risky. Failure is inevitable. Encourage your people to fail fast. As Thought Leaders founder Matt Church puts it, *"Failure is not OK, but we need to get OK with failure"*. A lot of change resistance is fear-based – some rational, some not. Fear of failure is a big contributor, so creating a positive attitude to failure will accelerate your rate of change!

4. *Don't let planning get in the way of doing.*
   May businesses either under or over-plan their change projects. Get on with it. Mastering agility and developing an ability to get stuff done in an uncertain environment is key to giving people the confidence they need to thrive in our new world of pretty much continuous change.

5. ***Understand that progress is the most powerful motivator in getting change done***
   We're human. We don't thrive on repetitive tasks that make us feel stuck like hamsters on a wheel. Make change meaningful. Let us know why we are doing it (in terms that matter to us) and how we're going. Do this well and do it often and chances are you will win the change game.

Little of this is new of course. What is new is the urgency. If the mantra of change is coming from the top office, chances are this is now mainstream. Those that master change win. The rest… not so much! Bob Dylan had it right…

> *Come gather 'round people*
> *Wherever you roam*
> *And admit that the waters*
> *Around you have grown*
> *And accept it that soon*
> *You'll be drenched to the bone.*
> *If your time to you*
> *Is worth savin'*
> *Then you better start swimmin'*
> *Or you'll sink like a stone*
> *For the times they are a-changin'.*

What do you think?

Why blogging is an essential weapon in activating Brand You

I first wrote *'the blog about my blog'* 2 years ago. I wanted to lift the bonnet on *'Pinch of Thought'* to show how it actually works and why. My premise – that writing a blog is no longer a nice-to-do, but a business essential. The intervening 24 months have deepened this belief. You see 'content creation' is an increasingly important part of the connection puzzle. Last week I wrote about the Gig Economy and how we need to create our own personal brand equity to avoid the commoditization of our expertise. Content creation and sharing via a simple blog is still the best way to get started. It's not new, but the likelihood is that you are not doing it. I've heard all of the excuses ("too busy", "too hard", "it doesn't work") – and that is all they are.

Blogging is a low cost, efficient and even enjoyable way to connect with your market, develop and display your thinking and simply remind people that you still exist! It's about helping people and in the process starting a conversation that may – or may not – become commercial. Importantly, you must be genuinely happy with either.

So here's a bit of a refresh on how it works and why I reckon it's now imperative that you get onto this.

FIRST LET'S DE-BUNK SOME MYTHS
No one is waiting for your blog. No one will call to say they haven't received it (well, your mum might). You are unlikely to be inundated with an avalanche of sales enquiries seconds after you press SEND. Indeed, often you will give digital life to your painfully-crafted wisdom and receive in thanks a deafening silence…

So is it all a giant con? Has your reluctance to jump on the content creation bandwagon been vindicated? Are we bloggers just spinning our wheels?

SORRY, BUT THE ANSWER IS NO!
Like most things in today's ambiguous world, binary answers don't serve. It's too easy to say the blogs are a waste of time (or that social media or online marketing doesn't work). It's simplistic, lazy and just not true. They all work, but you have to learn how and adapt accordingly.

HOW BLOGS REALLY WORK TO DRIVE YOUR BUSINESS
Make no mistake. Your blog has the potential to become a veritable Energizer bunny for your business. I find it works in a few ways:

1. *A consistent reminder to your customers (existing and potential) that you are out there and active*
   Your customers are unlikely to work with people and businesses they don't know. You don't, I don't, so it's nuts to expect any differently just because it's our 'brilliance' on display. Like a personal relationship, it takes time to build trust. Through your blog, you will often be creating impact without knowing it. It's likely that only a few readers will respond when you post, but many more are reading and forming a positive view that may later convert into business. I invariably find that the first time most of my clients experience me is through my blog, which they've been silently consuming, often for 6, 12 or 18 months before making contact.

2. *A permission-based vehicle for you to showcase how you can help your clients solve their most pressing problems*
   Remember, at some stage, readers have elected to let you into their inbox. That's a precious thing and the starting point for

a great relationship if what you offer is what your customers need.

3. ***A brilliant format through which you can test and evolve your thinking, services and products***
Blogs are a great way to trial ideas with your market. They're a perfect vehicle to build a client community around your concepts and to start conversations that will help you better-understand needs and opportunities. The best blogs are brief and informal. They are the equivalent of a café chat, not a boardroom pitch.

4. ***An elegant prompt to remind customers to get in touch***
After I post my blog, I usually get a lot of emails about unconnected conversations that are in play. The blog acts as a gentle prompt that saves me having to follow up (which can appear needy) and keeps projects moving.

SOME BLOG RULES I'VE FOUND HELPFUL

1. *Great content is essential*
Without good content, you ARE wasting your time. For any leaders, entrepreneurs and experts who struggle with this I run several individual and group programmes, so please get in touch below.

2. *Be consistent and persistent (post at least every 2 weeks)*
Ever had an unreliable friend – one who turns up late or just doesn't show? It's hard to build a trusting relationship with someone like that and definitely a bad look for a business. Your blog has to show up like clockwork. Even if it's not opened (and expect that most won't be), your customer will know that you are still alive and kicking. Subconsciously they are assured

by your continuing activity.

1. **Be Patient**

   Do not expect fast, dramatic results. You blog is a powerful, but necessarily, slow-build strategy. It's like dropping pebbles in a pond. The ripples that your activity creates may take a long time to reflect back. But, if you are patient, they will – often from completely new and unexpected directions.

1. **Don't be boring**

   Take advantage of the less-formal nature of the blog format to find the voice that will really resonate with your customers. Avoid dry business language and cull all jargon and acronyms. ASAP!

1. **Have a point**

   Dare to have a point of view. Don't just refer to a new report or piece of research – tell your community what you think about it and what action they should take. There's no better place to develop your market thought leadership and influence.

1. **Don't sell**

   Use your blog to provide value, never to explicitly sell. Of course, you are selling all the time (this is a commercial activity after all), but you do it by attracting customers to what you do. They will come over time, but the choice is theirs. Your blog is there to provide value.

1. **Think multi media**

   I've described a traditional, written blog like Pinch of Thought, as it is the most common blog form and the most straightforward to create and distribute. Your blog can easily take other forms such as video, audio, infographics and slides.

Once you've mastered the basic form, it pays to play with re-purposing your content into these other formats.

And finally… have some fun
It's not War and Peace. Don't take yourself too seriously – I find self-deprecation is always appreciated)

BLOGS MAKE MONEY
My blog has led to at least $150,000 of billings for me in the last 12 months. I am a solo consultant – just me, my brilliant Business Manager, Kathryn, Muddy the dog and 2 cats.

Imagine what that could look like scaled up for your business – at virtually zero cost! If you are not harnessing the blog form, you are, at best, missing a trick and, at worst, leaving your business exposed as competitors fill the void left by your inactivity.

You know it's time. Get cracking, ignore the doubters and that little voice in your own head. Write something and JUST PRESS SEND. If you need a hand, just drop me a note.

Part 6: Self leadership

We constantly underestimate the cost of inaction.

— Margie Warell

Leadership lessons from a small boat

As someone who spends a lot of time working alone, I find it's important to stay connected. There's no natural water-cooler conversation in a one-man leadership consultancy and it's easy to become detached. We are social animals and need company to bring out the best in ourselves. We also need to work out physically to combat the effects of too much screen-time and too little activity.

I've found the perfect outlet in the sport of surfboat rowing. Surfboats are 8 metres-long and carry 4 rowers and a 'sweep', who steers (and shouts!). They're raced in carnivals with 6 boats at a time competing in an out-and-back course of 800metres. I joined a Masters crew in early 2016 and learned quickly of the dangers, leaving my second carnival in an ambulance. This is a tough sport. As anyone who has taken on the ocean knows, there's only ever one winner. As an unknown poet wrote in a verse that graced the desk of President John F Kennedy:

Thy sea, O God, so great,
My boat so small,

Fast-forward a year and I'm back on the (sea)horse. My crew, the mighty Warriewood Crustys, is no longer making up the numbers. We've worked hard and are starting to be competitive. Along the way we've learned some great leadership lessons. I share them here.

PREPARATION COUNTS
The '7P's principle applies nowhere more than in a surfboat. *'Proper Prior Planning Prevents Piss-Poor Performance'*. Rowing is hard work. Many experts believe that Olympic rowers are the ultimate

athletes. Whilst we don't quite scale those heights, we train three times a week and endlessly rehearse the many technical aspects. There's a lot of hardware flying around and plenty of *"don't do that, stand there, sit here"* stuff to learn. This preparation, awareness and discipline is exactly the stuff required of strong leadership teams.

ALL FOR ONE AND ONE FOR ALL

Collaboration in teams is much-vaunted, but often little-seen. We've been taught to compete rather than collaborate. I do a lot of my mentoring work helping leaders to develop a genuinely collaborative intent and capability.

In a surfboat there's no choice. It's one of the ultimate collaborative experiences as the actions of one person will significantly disrupt the collective effort. A missed-stroke, poor timing or a delay in reacting to whatever the ocean is throwing up can result in anything from reduced boat speed to spectacular failure (read swimming!).

A MARATHON NOT A SPRINT

When I started rowing, I thought the event was a sprint. So I pulled like a maniac out to the turning buoy… and then faded horribly, exhausted. I now know it is more like an 800 metre run. Effort must be measured, conserved and then expended at just the right time.

It's the same with team performance. We can't be incessantly running at full tilt. I remember a weekly sales meeting from years ago. Every Monday it was a 'big week'. We had to smash targets. After a while I realized these were unachievable. The motivational speech was anything but… yet, used sparingly, I don't doubt it could have been effective.

A TIME TO GO! AND A TIME TO WAIT

If the waves are big, the strategy must shift – from progress to survival. Once the starting gun goes, we may get off the beach and then stop and hold position, waiting for a slight pause in the waves. Either side, competing crews may take a chance, rushing heroically into the oncoming breakers. It's easy to feel we are missing out, that we've made a mistake. Sometimes they get through, but, more often, they get stopped by the first wave and then – stuck in the wrong place at the wrong time – smashed by the second. Having waited, we then choose the right moment to 'GO', get through the break and carry on racing.

Leadership is not about unceasingly moving forward. Sometimes it's knowing when to do nothing, to wait-out adverse conditions or allow earlier efforts to take effect. We rely on our sweep to call the shots (fortunately, as rowers face backwards, we can't see what's coming!). A great leader must demonstrate the same skills – based on deep market knowledge, good instinct and a comprehensive understanding of the teams' capability.

MOTIVATION COMES IN MANY FORMS

Above all, we're in a race. The idea is to win, to expend every ounce of available energy just as the boat crosses the finishing line, surfing on a victory wave. That's the aim anyway. Extracting said effort is an art-form. Again, the sweep drives everything. Strategies range from encouragement: *"come on, we're placed second, one boat-length back, give me 5 big ones"*, to fear: *"you better pull us onto this wave 'cos that big one behind is gonna hit us up the arse if you don't"*.

As leaders, there IS a place for both the carrot and the stick!

HAVE A SECRET WEAPON OR TWO!

Any team needs a special sauce, something that bonds them

culturally. Teams work best with a smile. Our special sauce looks like this! We're not sure whether competitors are put off with fear, pity or laughter, but we like them!

BE PART OF SOMETHING BIGGER THAN MONEY OR YOURSELF
As important at the competition is, the thing I love even more about surfboat rowing is the people and community. These are 'get-shit-done' folk. It's amazing to see an empty beach transformed within a couple of hours to a carnival of boats, tents, people and racing. It's the kind of thing that would take a council several days and many hi-viz vests to 'manage'.

There's also a great sense of tradition and respect that unites crews ranging from under-19 male and females to gnarly old masters in their 70s. The love of the ocean and of the tradition of the sport is still strong. It's seen at its finest when passing greats are honoured in a moving, oars-raised ceremony.

In 2017, that's a rare and precious thing.

The Crusty Crew is off in pursuit of State glory at the weekend. With a fair wind and special sauce, who would bet against us?

The world needs you! Are you ready?

Funny how some things just stick in your head. I can always remember that the axial tilt of the earth is 23.5 degrees. I can't remember much else (and often swap the name of my dog and my sixteen year old son when shouting at either), but 23.5 degrees – that's for life.

I mention this, because in 2016, I think the earth shifted. Not physically, but certainly metaphorically. A lot of things I've been thinking and writing about for several years have come sharply into focus. Now I'm not claiming savant qualities – it's just in my game of personal and business transformation, you need to look ahead. I find it rather useful. I am also constantly surprised that many of the leaders who one would expect to be similarly occupied, appear to be looking more at their boots than the horizon.

That's both puzzling and dangerous.

So, in the spirit of the end of year, here are a few trends I see for 2017.

THE DEATH OF THE EXPERT

Brexit and Trump. The pundits, the economists, the markets the media and even the bookies got it wrong. Completely, stone-cold, 100 per cent wrong. That's damning and illustrates the danger we all face in living in our own little echo chambers of self-interest and bias. It's getting harder to get our heads up and see what's going on, but, make no mistake, the treasure will go to those who do.

As Oscar Wilde observed,

> *We are all in the gutter, but some of us are looking at the stars.*

THOUGHT LEADERS MUST STEP UP
Apparently we are now post-truth. This was brazenly demonstrated in Australia when the Labour party's 'Mediscare' lie was texted to thousands of voters on election-day. It's dispiriting that democracy has become so debased.

Far from 'keeping 'em honest', the media is a big part of the problem. So much content is now advertiser-supplied or sponsored and (as we saw on the Trump election) even the supposedly neutral news chairs are heavily biased. The legendary anchors of Christmas past (Walter Kronkite, Richard Dimbleby and Brian Henderson) would be appalled.

I see no fix for the end of intelligent, ethical and balanced debate in a public sense. Privately however, it creates greater opportunity and responsibility for the independent thought leaders who, looking beyond self-interest, can show us the way to create a better collective future.

WHITE COLLAR JOBS ARE BEING COMMODITIZED
I am unexcited by the glitzy new 'hubs' popping up all over town. The promise of open-plan working for independent portfolio workers who can network and collaborate with fast wi-fi and complimentary coffee may become the C21 version of Dickensian factory working. Not all bad of course, but best approached with caution.

Combine this with the rise of agencies like Expert 360 that matches organizations with the experts they need on a project basis (e.g. CIO, CFO, Change lead) and you can see how the value of those same experts is likely to be eroded in a race-to-the-bottom. Both models are great news – for the landlords and the portal owners. But for experts who see this as a new way to get work without having to sell themselves, I fear there may be trouble ahead. Far better to build your own reputation and influence as a thought leader to win the work you want on your own terms.

LEADERS ARE LOST

As I write, Tim Worner, the CEO of Seven West Media is mired in a sex and drugs scandal and the Board is struggling to come to the bewilderingly obvious and ethical solution. Meanwhile, Eddie Obeid is contemplating Christmas at Her Majesty's Pleasure and IMF Chief Christine Lagarde has been found guilty on criminal charges of misuse of public funds (oh the irony!). Sadly, we are not surprised. Leadership is in crisis.

There are many people who confuse being in a leadership position with being a leader. There's a big difference! And the clock is ticking for those who cannot or will not step up. To win in today's challenging business environments, we need leaders who are empathetic, agile, attuned and humble. We need leaders who set a clear vision, communicate it brilliantly and put themselves last on the journey to getting there. When these people deliver, magic happens. I think we'll see a big shift as businesses finally understand that they must change what they are looking for in their leaders – at both business and Board level. The old world of pale, male, stale time-servers is up.

THE MOVE TO A UNIVERSAL WAGE

We will see a lot more discussion about how we must rethink work and reward. Millions of manual jobs are disappearing and, as Tim Dunlop argues in his excellent book, 'Why the future is Workless', most will not be replaced. The implications are massive. The transition is likely to be very painful and messy. It's part of the Trump story, but only the start. Many currently successful, employed people are likely to lose out and spend their retirement in relative poverty. Positioning ourself to remain relevant and valuable through that change requires work and investment. Don't worry, it's rewarding in every sense. Doing nothing is a sure path to unhappiness.

WHAT WILL YOU DO?

As we look into 2017, I find myself positively agitated. I worry about the world and the direction it is taking. Change abounds and it's not all good. But I am buoyed by the opportunity to work with others to see what we can do about it all. There are many amazing opportunities and I have seen the extraordinary results that individuals and teams who decide to 'lean in' can create.

I believe it's a time for us all to step up. More-of-the-same is won't serve either ourselves or others. So I am in.

What will you do?

Time to get our brains in the game

I recently had to re-paint the woodwork on my deck. It was covered in dust and loose paint, so I knew I needed to first clean off the dirt then rub it down with sandpaper. In other words, I prepared. I knew that missing these steps would result in a bodge job that would look terrible and soon need re-doing.

Similarly, when we go to the gym, or get ready for a sport, we prepare our bodies by warming up. When we don't, we know we'll feel terrible and are prone to injury (especially if, like me, your lycra-wearing days are behind you!) Again, we know we need to get our bodies ready to maximise our chances of success.

So far so what? We all know this stuff and either do it – or know we should! By contrast, most of us give little thought to **mentally** preparing ourselves to perform at work. Driven by unquestioned rituals (e.g. meetings) and processes, we rush unthinkingly from one task to the next. So a meeting with our boss is followed by a staff review, then some customer calls and finally some report writing. Each of these requires different things of our brain. We should create a space to consider, pause, reflect and mentally prepare for each. Instead we rush on in a misguided belief that we are being productive. In reality, we're slapping on the paint and turning up to play 5 minutes before kick off. High time then that we gave more thought to building our mental readiness.

Mental Readiness is one of the four pillars of the Performance Competency in the i4 Neuroleader model:

Integration
Balance

Ethics
Mental Readiness

Mental Readiness refers to the ability of a person to create a balanced psychological state in which they can perform at an optimal level. It's about mastering the capacity to focus, self-manage and maintain a healthy degree of internal discipline to approach (and enjoy) the challenge ahead.

In turn, Mental Readiness is made up of three elements:

Confidence
Focus
Planning
Confidence

In business, people value and encourage confidence in themselves and others in an often casual or random fashion. This is strange given how positively we view confidence (but not arrogance) in our leaders. Conversely, most of us have worked with colleagues who are, often inexplicably to us, stricken with a lack of confidence that completely overrides their ability to get the best from themselves.

As Vince Lombardi – the highly successful American Football coach who led the Green Bay Packers to five NFL championships in seven years – said:

> *Confidence is contagious. So is lack of confidence.*

Building confidence is often a matter of awareness. It is easy to obsess on our failings and devalue the many counter-balancing successes. When we run workshops at About My Brain Institute, one exercise unfailingly reveals that most of us feel inadequate – at least some of the time. Good leaders know the importance of nurturing confidence – both in themselves and others – to counter this deep seated 'not good enough' paradigm. Helping someone in your team to overcome a confidence deficit to unlock their potential not only feels wonderful – it's great for business too.

FOCUS

The single biggest challenge of the contemporary work environment is in conditioning ourselves to overcome distraction. Emails, chat heads, texts, ubiquitous screens and 24/7 connection are hard to ignore. Perhaps our brains work against us here, by offering those little dopamine hits when we are stimulated by a new piece of information. Add in the trend to open-plan offices – that aim to encourage and facilitate collaboration, but for many have created impossibly distraction-heavy environments – and it's easy to see why we struggle to focus for prolonged periods.

Both intentionally and unintentionally, our response is often to withdraw. That's why it's not unusual to see people walking in the street oblivious to those around them, or co-workers with far-away eyes, escaping into their noise-cancelling headphones.

This is a problem and, unsurprisingly, has significant impact on individual and team performance. We must learn to be fully-present – both to perform at our best in any given task, but also so that we are effective when interacting with others. Building our focus can provide us with greater information recall and a more stable mood – both pre-requisites of good leadership. Mindfulness techniques and neuro-measurement devices are different approaches to helping us win the focus game.

PLANNING

We know that planning is important, but so often, under the

pressure to "get stuff done", succumb to winging it. The satisfaction of feeling we are progressing with a task is quickly replaced by frustration once we realise we have not planned well and are wasting time and resources.

With this in mind, there is a lot that we can do to better access the most productive parts of our brains to bring to bare on the task. Activities can include:

- Visualising a situation and its probably outcomes before it happens.
- Physically preparing by breathing and centering.
- Reinforcing other people's thoughts through words (the half-time peptalk!).
- Breaking a task down into smaller chunks – particularly useful if it is complex

Proper planning helps the executive part of our brain to think more clearly and prepares it to better deal with the unknown and unknowable.

As leaders, it's smart to invest time in these planning activities before we jump into execution. So writing what needs to be communicated, mentally rehearsing a difficult conversation or talking through a presentation and anticipating likely questions are all great ways to increase performance and reduce anxiety.

My favourite planning quote is by Abraham Lincoln, who said:

> *Give me six hours to chop down a tree and I will spend the first four sharpening the axe.*

For most of us, it's a case of more sharpening and less swinging!

GET AHEAD BY GETTING MENTALLY READY

When we stop to think about the significant personal and performance upsides to be gained by investing even a small amount of time in building our mental readiness, it's a no-brainer. In a competitive world, it may just be the difference between success and failure.

Everyone's got a plan until they get punched in the face

I love this quote by former world heavyweight boxer, Mike Tyson. Whether you love or loathe 'the noble art', as a man who won his first nineteen fights with knockout punches, 'Iron Mike' clearly knew a bit about disrupting the best made plans of wannabe world champs. And – whilst few would argue he's a great thinker – we can learn a lot from his blunt assessment.

GOTTA GET UP AGAIN
As part of the Thought Leaders community, I help clever people to become commercially smart. This takes many forms. I share a fantastic curriculum, help students get to grips with high-performance tools and wield the carrot & stick of accountability. One of the most valuable aspects though is to help people to understand the fight they are in. Be under no illusions. If you plan to stand out as an influencer and make a good living doing so, you are up for your fair share of failure and pain.

WEBINAR WOES
About a year ago, I remember running a webinar on Building your success plan. I had over 50 great people online and ready to roll. When zero hour came, however, I couldn't get the technology to work. After 15 agonizing minutes, I had to abandon and re-schedule. PUNCH 1. Despite testing and rehearsal I felt like an amateur. It turned out the gazillion dollar platform had a 'server error' and they were 'sorry!!!!'. I was fuming. Even when we re-did it, there were more glitches, fewer attendees and sound only on the live feed. PUNCH 2. We kind of got there in the end, but it was not a confidence-inspiring experience. It was in the middle of the Australian summer and by the end, I looked and felt like I'd done

a couple of rounds with Iron Mike.

LEARN HOW TO TAKE A PUNCH

In the early stages of our development, it is easy to let this stuff smash our confidence and derail our focus and productivity in a big way. We tend to amplify our own importance in the minds of others. The truth is, most people just don't care. Not in a nasty way, but simply because they are too busy. People know that technology stuffs up and projects fail. I find they are actually remarkably forgiving and generous.

5 TIPS TO GETTING OFF THE ROPES FAST

So the trick is not to avoid getting punched – that's unavoidable. It's to take the punch, shake it off and press on undeterred. Here are a few ideas to get you back in the fight.

Understand that failure is a part of the journey

The simple acceptance that we are going to fail and it will hurt when we do is great preparation. It's reality and the price of freeing ourselves from the paralysis of perfection.

Plan to fail

At Thought Leaders we take this idea further. We actually plan to fail in 50% of what we do. The workshop we put on doesn't get enough interest? Fail it. Not enough sales for a new program? Fail it. These are still punches and they still hurt. But by acknowledging up front that this will happen we minimize the disruption to our flow (usually caused by us personalizing the failure in to some form of 'I am not good enough').

Test early

Whilst we are going to get punched, we can be smart about minimizing the impact. We need to prototype – to test the viability and demand for our commercial ideas as early as possible. So we run a pilot program (acknowledging that it's not fully polished) or publish a test chapter. Adopting this approach prevents us from investing any more time that we have to in finding out if our offering will fly or flop.

Get sequence in your camp

If you are going to take on Mike Tyson, you'll want to work your way up through a program of training in which you build your skills, resilience, strength and tactics. In the same way, we need to start with the appropriate projects for our level of experience. For example, I always encourage people to start authoring blogs before they take on longer white papers and ultimately books. There is a lot of bad information out there that encourages relative novices to write a book – TODAY! If you are just starting out that's a bad plan (the equivalent of jumping into the ring with the Champ on day 1). Your ideas are only partly formed and no one knows who you are. Even if you do manage to write a good book, no one will care. You'll have wasted a ton of time, resources and emotional energy in an activity that is out of sequence.

Get a community of great seconds in your corner

As ever, it pays to laugh at your trials and tribulations. Find a community of like-minded folk to share your fight club stories with. Believe me, you'll find everyone has endured the punches. It will get you match fit more quickly and help maintain that healthy dose of perspective that we all need.

So time to step into the ring and 'plan for pain'. It will probably do you the world of good.

Ready to grow? Get a mentor who's in your camp (and in your face!)

I recently refreshed the testimonials for one of my mentoring programmes. I was surprised to discover that I've helped over 40 clever people to grow their income, influence, confidence and happiness in the last two years. This week, I explore some ideas around why I believe smart players need a great mentor.

MY FIRST MENTORING EXPERIENCE

I remember vividly my own first experience of working with a mentor. It says a lot about my own ignorance (and the lack of investment in 'talent' in the media industry where I worked for 20 years) that I was 40 when this life-changing event occurred.

You see I'd been cruising. I'd done well in various leadership roles, smashed my targets and was generally perceived (and thought of myself) as a high performer. I'd had enough of the media industry and was in the final round of interviewing for a role leading a business turnaround at a large Australian not-for-profit. I was to meet with an external guy named Paul for a final check. Expecting a polite 'box-ticking' chat, I was shocked when said Paul jumped all over my resume and, metaphorically, me. He asked why I hadn't done more, studied more, grown more, challenged myself more and – ultimately – achieved more!

Whilst this may sound like a brutal and unfair experience, it was actually cathartic. Paul was one shrewd cookie. He saw straight through me and spoke many truths – some hard and some inspiring. For the first time in a long time, I felt challenged and excited. I remember leaving the grilling in a state of agitation and sat in my car afterwards writing down as much as I could remember of what

Paul had said. I must have done something right because I got the job.

A few months later, my new boss said I should get a mentor. His name was Paul! Over the next year we worked on growing both myself and the business I led. I was introduced to new ways of thinking and being and was encouraged to start an MBA. I learned more in that 12+ months than I had in the previous 10 years. I loved it. What I learned working with my mentor was a big factor in why I was able to lead my team to achieve extraordinary success.

RIGHT FOR YOU?

If you've never had a mentor, it's time you did! If you are a leader, chances are you will have received at least some level of formal leadership training. That's great, but the demands of our fast-change VUCA world mean you will benefit far more from a bespoke approach. If you work for yourself, it's just as important to have someone to help keep you inspired, accountable and on-track.

7 QUALITIES TO LOOK FOR IN A GREAT MENTORING RELATIONSHIP

Finding the right mentor is hugely important. Look for someone who is:

1. *Expert*

    The main difference between mentoring and coaching is that a mentor has expertise in a specific area. For example, I mentor experts to build their influence for professional and commercial success and also leaders to drive transformational change. I have specific expertise and experience in both of these domains. It's vital to ensure that your mentor has the requisite expertise to stretch and guide your development. As Peter Drucker wrote,

No one learns as much about a subject as one who is forced to teach it.

2. **Inspiring**

    The outcomes that flow from a great mentoring relationship can be extraordinary. Part of this comes from what the mentor can see in you that you can't see yourself. My favourite definition of a leader is of "one who brings out greatness in others". So it is with mentoring. Your mentor must have an abundant and optimistic view for your future possibilities – and the skill and tools to help you unlock them.

3. **Authentic**

    Sadly, this term has become overused, but it's critical in a mentor. This is an intimate relationship, based on trust. To get the best results, you will need to make yourself open and vulnerable – to share your thoughts, aspirations and fears? For that to happen you will need a mentor who is completely up-front, honest and clear about how the relationship is to work. If you don't sense this is the case, keep looking!

4. **Honest**

    At times brutally! An extension of authenticity, a mentoring relationship should be stretching and encouraging. Total honesty and commitment on both sides is vital to ensuring that progress is maintained and any diversions are quickly addressed. There will be tensions – and that's a good thing.

5. **Bold**

    We live in an age that demands courage and experimentation. It's likely there are few easy answers in your world, so you need a mentor who will encourage you to be bold. As, William Murray wrote, "Boldness has genius, power, and magic in it!"

A good mentor will challenge your assumptions and help you to consider new ideas, actions and possibilities. This is not – and should not be – a safe and predictable process. Expect to be disturbed – in a good way.

6. *Impatient*
You will be busy and have many competing calls on your time and attention. Mentoring relationships typically concentrate on bigger picture issues, behaviours and outcomes. It's easy to allow the 'noise' of daily work to detract from your focus. A good mentor will keep you on track, insisting that you deliver against apparently impossible deadlines. It's amazing what we can achieve when pushed. As a result you will achieve strategic shifts that create new paradigms when you move to higher level of thinking and operating.

7. *Connected*
A good business mentor should have a clear commercial focus for you. As part of this, they will be connected with the people, resources, tools and networks that you will need to advance. In this sense, business mentoring is quite different to an academic relationship. It must be much more than a knowledge transfer.

HOW MUCH DOES IT COST?

Expect to pay $15,000–$30,000+ for a year of mentoring. Some specialists will command a lot more. Whether this is a good investment depends on where you are 'at' and what you are trying to achieve. I believe too many people place a blind faith in, for example, MBA programmes. These cost a lot more (in AU an average of $44,000 and up to $81,000) and involve a greater time commitment. They enjoy an academic (and social) respectability and offer an implied value through enhanced earning potential. I'm not so sure – certainly not for everyone. In the rapidly changing world of work, highly-paid executive roles are under threat and salaries are flat-lining. The evidence to support a return on investment appears ironically anecdotal.

GIVE IT A SHOT

A good mentoring relationship will provide the highly-customized approach and inherent agility that implies. It should also be tightly focused on delivering the agreed outcomes and ideally repay the investment during the term of the engagement. That's certainly the way I operate. If you've never had a mentor, it's a good idea to give it a go. I know my first mentor helped to super-accelerate my performance and personal growth. I just wish I had started sooner.

▰▰▰ Are you playing in the right space?

I am a big rugby union fan. At the weekend, England took on the un-fancied Italians in their annual 6 Nations competition fixture. The 'Azzuri' excel in coffee, cuisine and love, but the expectation was for an easy win for the competition leaders. Whilst they ultimately prevailed, it wasn't without drama. The Italians exploited rule technicalities that enabled their players to position themselves in unexpected places. The English were clearly confused. Their advantage in power, player quality and financial resources (England being by far the wealthiest rugby union) was neutralised. The clever Italian tactics forced them back time and again. They were playing in the wrong space.

THE GAME HAS CHANGED

As leaders, we need to make sure we are not similarly distracted. I believe too many businesses allow their leaders to focus on the wrong things. They get pulled into (or find comfort in) day-to-day detail and become lost in management. In our fast-changing business world, that's a recipe for disaster. Successful leaders must be focused on the bigger-picture, obsessed with answering two questions. Where are going? How will we get there?

My model below explains:

ARE YOU PLAYING IN THE RIGHT SPACE?

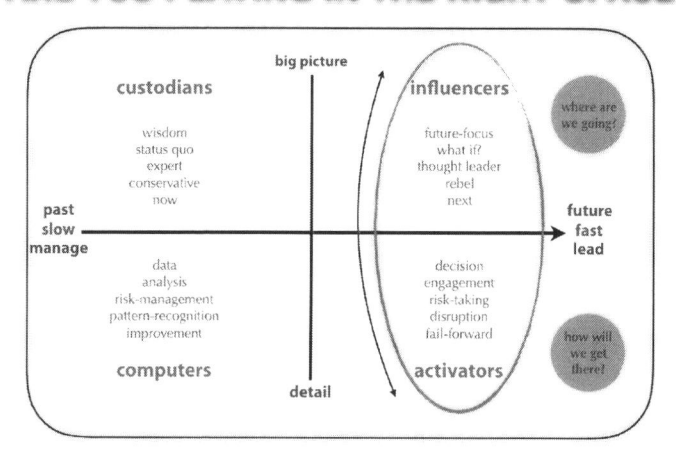

```
                          big picture
        custodians           |      influencers
                             |                        where are
              wisdom         |       future-focus     we going?
              status quo     |       what if?
              expert         |       thought leader
              conservative   |       rebel
              now            |       next
  past  ─────────────────────┼─────────────────────── future
  slow                       |                        fast
  manage                     |                        lead
              data           |       decision
              analysis       |       engagement
              risk-management|       risk-taking
              pattern-recognition|   disruption       how will
              improvement    |       fail-forward     we get
                             |                        there?
        computers            |      activators
                          detail
```

mark HODGSON

The vertical axis of the model is about focus and ranges from 'detail' to the 'big picture'. The horizontal axis indicates 3 continua. 'past' to 'future', 'slow' to 'fast' and 'manage' to 'lead'. Stick with me and I'll explain. This creates 4 quadrants. Where should you be playing?

COMPUTERS
The bottom left quadrant. Detail-heavy tasks, based on current and past activity, are best performed by computers. Software, technology and artificial intelligence are now supremely capable at analyzing and extrapolating information for improving efficiencies. If you are spending a lot of time in this space, chances are you'll soon be replaced by a machine!

CUSTODIANS
Of course you do need to keep an eye on current business performance – at a big picture, strategic level. You must be in the 'now'. Here you are custodian of the business and the brand. It's about using your expertise and wisdom to maintain the status quo in

a predictable, conservative manner. Shareholders and the market don't like surprises. The problem is that, for many, leadership stops here. It's necessary but not sufficient. Successful leaders must look, think and act beyond the present.

INFLUENCERS

Smart leaders have to build their influence. Influence is a new source of personal and organizational power. As the rate of change accelerates beyond our ability to keep up, we are looking for answers. We seek out the thought leaders who can tell us what will happen and how we can position ourselves to succeed. You will be future-focused, fascinated with creating the 'next'. You must cast off the shackles of conservatism and rebel. The future is likely to come from unexpected directions, so you need to challenge the status quo and push your thinking into new areas. You must also communicate your vision – to the business, to customers and the broader market. In doing so, you inspire confidence and attract new partners. This is where influencers create commercial advantage as the money follows the ideas.

ACTIVATORS

As exciting as the 'influencer' role is, it's not the complete story. The best leaders must also activate. That's about building the plan and resources to create the future you see. Making decisions. Switching from risk-management to risk-taking. Disrupting what already exists in the business and motivating and engaging the staff to want to go on the journey.

It's not enough to be a futurist with a helicopter view. Today's leaders must play in both the 'influencer' and 'activator' space – shifting between the big picture vision and the 'boots-on-the-ground detail needed to bring it about.

WHERE ARE YOU PLAYING?

Are you focused in the past? Stuck in the slow lane? Merely managing people and processes? If you are in a leadership role, that's not enough. It may have been in the past , but not now. You are not creating enough value to secure your future. It's time to speed up, to become more agile, to look to what may be and stick your neck out in the process of creating it. There's risk of course, but leaders are in the risk-taking business. Better to fail-forward today than fail-completely tomorrow.

Playing in the wrong place almost caused the England rugby team to fail in what was meant to be their easiest game of the season. Ultimately, they adapted to the new paradigm and prevailed. They evolved and won.

Have you?

Times are a changin' – and so must we

We all know that change is here and accelerating. It's impossible to keep up with everything and easy to become overwhelmed. At times, giving up even trying can be tempting. Tempting, but a big mistake. Staying current is one of the most important skills we need to develop. Even better, if we can get out ahead of the change wave, we can create the space to stand out commercially and the time to enjoy the journey.

FAST OR SLOW?
First we must get up to speed. We need to work out who is moving fastest in our world and make sure we're running at that pace. The good news is that scale is no barrier to speed. Ironically – it's often the incumbent sector leaders who struggle, outmanoeuvred by smaller, more agile players. I was reminded of this in three recent events I attended.

OLD SCHOOL
The first was a presentation by an internationally renowned professor at an event promoted by Australia's leading business school. The talk was about *'Thriving through disruption'* (very much my bag). I was excited… and then disappointed. It was terrible. The thinking was textbook stale, the case studies tired and the big and interesting questions ducked. There was nothing that couldn't have been gleaned from reading a paper. In other words, it was a waste of everyone's time. Oh, and the quality of the slides was appalling. Old fonts, dot points, poor design and crap images. I was embarrassed. The whole event was academic, self-congratulatory and complacent. What shocked me was that most of the attendees seemed to think it was OK! A room full of MBAs didn't get how

off the pace this was in so many ways.

OLD MEDIA

The second event was a gala review of 2016 by the *Sydney Morning Herald* for an audience of 1,500. Digital disruption has decimated the newspaper industry. Over the last decade, revenues have tumbled. The 'rivers of gold' have long dried up. Globally, proprietors have struggled to find a way to transition their masthead brands to make money in a me-too world of online platforms (many unpaid). Most, including Fairfax Media (owner of the SMH) have invested heavily in these digital platforms and the extraordinary options they offer in terms of graphics, content, video and audience customization. Against this backdrop, I was expecting something tight and visually stimulating from a showcase event. Instead we sat through a tired format of talking heads, static slides and 'celebrity' journos. It was conventional by any standards. Technically, there was nothing that couldn't have been presented ten years ago (and probably was!). For an iconic media company whose very survival depends on standing out in the new digital world that's a damning truth. That the average age of the audience was 55+ said it all. The next generation of customers was not in the room and probably never will be!

NEW DIRECTION

The third event was the latest immersion of the *Thought Leaders Business School*, of which I am a faculty member. For three days, a tribe of independent consultants, coaches and entrepreneurs came together – as we do quarterly. Whilst there is a brilliant guiding curriculum and process, the most remarkable thing is the 'speed' at which the room is moving. Picture 150 clever people in a laboratory of focused thinking and productivity. Ideas are formed, captured, combined and then placed into commercially smart propositions that customers will buy. We learn to test and fail. It's a rapid prototype approach and the quantity and quality of output is extraordinary. We also learn to present with a commitment to excellence. There's no excuse for poor presentations or average delivery. That these standards don't apply at a Fairfax or a leading university is indicative of how off the pace these institutions are (and one reason why both are under such challenge to stake their claim for relevance – even survival). At the end of the three days, the tribe disperses. Typically working alone and from home offices, they sell and deliver their state-of-the-art services to businesses of all sizes, staying connected as an online community. That's what agility now looks like and how change is harnessed for commercial success.

TIME TO PUT YOUR FOOT DOWN?
I make the point about TLBS not to promote it (though, please contact me to learn more), but to illustrate that we can all operate at the necessary speed to win in a fast-change world. It's a David and Goliath story and we, the 'small guys', can excel. There is a lot to it, but it IS possible.

5 IDEAS TO GET YOU MOVING

Fail fast
Not working? Admit it. Learn. Adapt. Move on.

Compress time
Guarding our time is vital to productivity. Avoid time-suck coffees, pointless meetings and vague projects. Minimize travel. Default to Skype meetings. Use tags and search functions to quickly access information. Set tight meeting parameters/outcomes and time limits.

Plug into leading thinkers in your field
A few key sites (e.g. HBR) and content aggregators (e.g. Scoop It) will generate all the information you need to look beyond the noise

of the status quo and think ahead of the rest.

Be playful
Change is chaotic, but also fun. Don't take it or you too seriously.

Find your Tribe
Find your own network of like-minded thinkers, supporters and collaborators. A key to both success and sanity!

READY TO REV UP?
Accelerating the pace at which you operate means less, not more work! Clarity is the key. Once we decide what we do, why and how, we can then stop doing all of the other things that create so much friction and waste time and energy. We can then focus on a much smaller area in which we can achieve mastery. We put change back in its box!

The future's already here – are you ready?

In 1993, American author and futurist William Ford Gibson observed that:

> *The future is already here, it's just not very evenly distributed.*

I was reminded of this on my recent trip to Nashville, where we stumbled across a vintage car exhibition. One of those wonderfully random happenings that rewards the curious traveler, I was blown away by the form and beauty of an array of vintage American and Italian classics. They were stunning and – even in today's terms – 'futuristic'. I was surprised to learn that most of the designs were over 50 years old. The picture above for example is of a 1955 Chrysler Ghia Gilda. Inspired by flight, rockets and the boundless optimism of post-war America (contrast that with today's nervy insecurity!), it was created 6 years before the first manned space flight, 14 years before Neil Armstrong's *'one giant leap'* and 16 years before the jumbo jet first entered commercial service.

PREDICTING THE FUTURE IS LESS IMPORTANT THAN BEING READY FOR IT

I was recently one of the keynote speakers at the 20th birthday celebration for Job Ready – a specialist software provider to the education and training sector that I work with. My fellow speakers were futurist Craig Rispin and Oli Moore from Facebook. Both painted pictures of extraordinary future possibilities, opportunities and challenges for the sector. Yet even these experts can only predict broad areas of development (e.g. the rise of artificial intelligence, nano-tech, third world connectivity) rather than specifics. There are simply so many variables, so much we don't know and can't predict.

For leaders and businesses, predicting the future is less important than being ready for it. We must equip ourselves for multiple eventualities and start to move in the most likely direction, even when we can't know the destination.

GETTING READY TO BOLDLY GO!
It's no secret that most of us struggle with change. When exposed to predictions about what the future may look like, we are as likely to be fearful as excited. I believe that ***bridging the gap between the known present and uncertain future is the most pressing challenge for leaders.***

Confronted by this, many leaders hide in day-to-day detail or rehash old solutions. For the most part they will fail. The challenges of rapid and disruptive change requires different things of us. We must develop new skills, attitudes and behaviours. When I speak about this, I am struck by how many senior folk nod in violent agreement… and then do nothing! They accept the premise yet don't believe it will apply to their industry or them personally.

As hope is not a great strategy, here are a few things we can do to give ourselves and our teams the best chance of success – today and tomorrow.

MIND THE GAP – 3 KEYS TO GETTING FUTURE FIT

1. *Become a change champion*
   If you accept that change is inevitable and accelerating, isn't it time to get out in front of it and lead the charge? I hate the term 'change management'. Change must be actively led – not passively 'managed'. As leaders, we're all now in the business

of change. Challenging the status quo, showing the way and motivating your people into action will serve you, them and your business well.

2. *Develop your thought leadership*
    The Job Ready event was a masterpiece in thought leadership by CEO, Marc Washbourne and his young team. Instead of just inviting 150 clients to a party, Marc took the opportunity to showcase the future direction for the business and sector by creating an event that challenged and inspired. The word 'software' and specific products names hardly featured. The thinking was at a higher-level; a conversation about strategic partnerships into the future, not products and prices. The beauty of adopting a thought leadership approach is that those transactions will happen anyway.

    Developing personal and corporate thought leadership is a high value, low cost way to stand out. Very few do it well. It remains a fantastic source of competitive advantage, whilst also forcing you to actively think about what's coming next.

3. *Rediscover your curiosity*
    One of the greatest challenges for older, established leaders is to find new approaches. Rather than reach into their bag of tricks for proven strategies that have worked in slower, more predictable times, leaders must become more curious. It's about:

    Experimentation (and the necessary acceptance of failure)
    Vulnerability (being comfortable saying *"I don't know – but let's find out"*)
    Democracy (understanding that good ideas exist everywhere in your business)

Most of all, it's about getting out of rigid habit. A re-invigorated sense of wonder and possibility married to years of experience and (hopefully) wisdom is a very powerful combination. It's also exactly what we need from our leaders.

ARE YOU READY?

There **are** contemporary versions of the stunning Chrylser Gia Gilder – in our immediate view and also in completely unrelated areas. As Gibson said, *"The future is here...."*

There **are** clues available as to what is coming. Our job is to lead ourselves and our teams to seek them out. We can then join-the-dots, prepare for what's next and take advantage before our competitors.

That's both a challenge and an opportunity. Are you ready?

Putting ethics at the centre of leadership

A visit to the website of the Ethics Centre in Sydney leads to a fantastic video telling us that "Ethics is at the Centre of Being Human". It details a range of areas to which ethics are central. *Birth, Right-to-Life, Identity, Love, Sex, Desire, Happiness, Belief, Gender, Bias, War…* The list is diverse and fascinating. I am struck by how little we generally think about ethics – at least consciously. In a world that many people feel is getting worse – one that has arguably lost its moral compass, I suspect and hope that this will change. When we see the Trumps, Clintons and Hanson's of our time effectively rewarded, despite advocating offensive positions and engaging in highly questionable, even illegal activities in their pursuit of power, one senses that it is time for a stronger stand to be made.

Ethics refers to the set of moral values and principles that guide our actions and enable us to distinguish between right and wrong. The act of reflecting and developing congruence across our values, emotions, thoughts and actions is critical if we are to lead effectively. In the Imagination Age, I believe the rise of ethical leaders will become a significant factor in what will make organisations successful (or not!). Younger workers in particular are motivated to seek out businesses that align with their values. As my friend, anthropologist Michael Hendersen writes, this generation is looking for *"Leaders worth following, Work worth doing and Cultures worth belonging to"*. This may be the dynamic that forces us all to pay more attention and 'walk' the ethics 'talk'.

Ethics is one of the four pillars of the Performance Competency in the i4 Neuroleader model, developed by Silvia Damiano of the About My Brain Institute. The pillars are:

Integration
Balance
Ethics and
Mental Readiness

In turn, Ethics consists of three elements:

Values
Judgment
Congruency

Values

Values seem very straight forward, yet it is telling how we can find our core beliefs challenged and distorted as leaders. This is most obvious on the public stage, where we see politicians contort and reverse their positions, often in clear contradiction to values they have previously claimed to be fundamental. Similarly there are notorious failures such as Enron, where values such as honesty and integrity were jettisoned in the pursuit of profit. Neuroscience studies suggest that the effect of greed on the brain is similar to that of drugs such as cocaine. This may explain why so many, already wealthy and successful, people keep driving for increasingly obscene rewards at any cost.

Whilst it is easy to point at others, it is instructive to ask of ourselves, *"Am I living my values?"* It is likely that incongruence with our values will, sooner or later, derail all of us. As Mahatma Gandi observed,

> *Your beliefs become your thoughts,*
> *Your thoughts become your words,*
> *Your words become your actions,*
> *Your actions become your habits,*

Your habits become your values,
Your values become your destiny.

Judgment

Judgment is the ability to perceive, understand, evaluate and make considered decisions. Poor judgment is associated with suboptimal functioning of the Pre-Frontal Cortex (PFC) – the part of our brain that is associated with higher order thinking and processing. Good judgment is naturally fundamental to good leadership.

In addition to potential problems with our PFC, it's likely that our judgment is affected by stress and fatigue. As leaders, we are tasked with making decision after decision and it can be exhausting. In our rush to just get through the volume of 'stuff' it's easy for our judgment to err – often without us realising (although others probably will). One solution is to check in with ourselves – to ask ourselves honestly, *"Am I making good decisions here, or just quick ones?"* It's also useful to give permission to our peers and reports (why not?) to positively challenge us. Done well, this helps to share the load, remind us to refresh and refuel (why hard decisions often seem so much easier the next morning) and ultimately to make more right calls, more often. As American author Will Rogers wryly observed.

Good judgment comes from experience, and a lot of that comes from bad judgment.

Congruency

It's well known the majority of our understanding comes not from what we hear, but what we see, feel and sense. For this reason, it's vital that we are congruent. Congruency implies that we say what we really mean, live what we believe and demonstrate consistency in our body language, tone of voice, facial expressions, attitudes and actions.

That's a long list. Both as leaders and as individuals it is easy for us to be incongruent – a little, or a lot. Unsurprisingly, mastering this is one of the keys to great leadership. When leaders genuinely model, demonstrate and embrace the values and behaviours that they espouse, they are likely to positively impact and inspire those around them to achieve extraordinary things.

Ethics then are both essential and – for many leaders, difficult to navigate. That noted, perhaps, we are guilty of over-thinking the complexities. As Mark Twain neatly put it:

When in doubt, tell the truth.

Why curiosity is the key to our future success

One of the emerging 'hot topics' of 2016 is the increasing awareness that computers and artificial intelligence are going to transform our world more rapidly and profoundly than we thought possible. Computers are learning to learn. They can already outsmart their human counterparts in winning at games like Chess and the (infinitely more complex) Chinese board game, Go. Books like *'The Rise of the Robots'* by Martin Ford predict that this will impact not just 'blue collar' jobs through automation (e.g. driverless trucks at mining sites), but also the professions, including medicine, law (insert your own lawyer joke here!) and accountancy. Other reports paint doomsday scenarios where millions of Australian jobs will disappear, with unconvincing assumptions that, as yet unknown, jobs will emerge to replace them.

The reality is that no one knows. What is certain is that things are changing fast – a trend is only going to accelerate. To succeed, we too must change. We must fight our fear – the base response that so many of us experience in response to the unknown. Instead, we must be courageous. Above all perhaps we need to be open to new possibilities. We must be Curious.

Curiosity is one of the 16 pillars of the i4 Neuroleader model. It sits within the competency of Innovation. The four pillars are:

Imagination
Drive
Curiosity
Attitude

Curiosity is not a word typically associated with business. We know that it killed the cat, but historically it hasn't been widely perceived as a source of profit, performance or differentiation. In the Imagination Age, I believe that must change. If we are to add value, to create and innovate in a world where, in one sense, we are competing with machines for our livelihood, curiosity becomes extraordinarily valuable.

In the model, Curiosity breaks down into 3 elements:

Eagerness to Learn
Inquisitive Nature
Honesty

Eagerness to Learn
As a leadership consultant I am constantly exasperated that organisations employing hundreds or thousands of people, with annual salary bills of many $Millions put aside so little to invest in this precious (and costly) resource. It's like buying a Ferrari and then saying you can't afford the petrol to run it. Smart leaders create a culture of learning, experimentation and growth and insist that the business invests. Last-year-plus-a-bit-thinking is guaranteed to fail, so we need to look for new information, ideas and partnerships.

In the Information Age, knowledge itself was power. In the Imagination Age, the value (and power) now comes from the application of knowledge in new and creative ways. Leaders must take every opportunity to learn and also to encourage their people to seek out new knowledge. So don't just attend your annual industry event, send staff to different marketplaces and online knowledge waterholes. TED-style events are a great example. Give your staff a personal development budget and task them to come back with a 12-month plan for their development. You might be amazed by where their curiosity will lead them and your business.

Inquisitive Nature
As leaders, it is easy to remain in our comfort zone, where we know the territory and are confident of the answers. We must ask more questions. Asking questions and demonstrating an inclination to investigate are essential ingredients of curiosity. It often starts with challenging our well-worn habits and rituals. Ideas to kick-start change include reading a book in a new topic area, visiting a new town or country and listening to a different genre of music.

We can all become stuck. The days when we would work for just a handful of companies across several decades are well and truly gone. If we are to rise to the challenge and compete personally and professionally in a world of intelligent design computers, we have to force ourselves to evolve and adapt. We must learn to revel in *"I don't know", but I'd love to find out"*.

Honesty
Perhaps a surprising quality to be associated with innovation, honesty is fundamental to our ability to give our all. Research by behavioural economist Dan Ariely found the possibility of losing increases our motivation to cheat and ignore out ethics. The coming changes caused by the explosion in artificial intelligence and related technologies are likely to test us to the core. Indeed, Hamish Douglass, CEO of the influential Magellan Financial Group predicts the impact could be greater than the industrial revolution.

To move forward then, we must prize honesty and openness. The alternative creates weak cultures of mistrust and self-interest. Clearly, we will need to be at our ethical best to empower our curiosity. In turn, this will lead to the new discoveries, ideas and partnerships that await for those who get this right.

American poet E.E Cummings wrote that:

Once we believe in ourselves, we can risk curiosity, wonder, spontaneous delight, or any experience that reveals the human spirit.

As with the industrial revolution, there will be big winners and losers in the coming 'Artificial Intelligence' revolution. As leaders, we have to lean in. We must learn to use our extraordinary brains in new ways. As Cummings observes, we must "believe in ourselves". Nurturing our curiosity and going where it takes us is the very DNA of this process.

Now let's all go have an adventure…

My first year on the Lifeline

Warning: In this blog, I discuss my volunteer work at Lifeline, Australia's leading support agency for people in crisis, including those contemplating suicide. If this is a painful or difficult issue for you, please skip this Pinch of Thought. Thanks, Mark.

I was recently inundated by a mail storm of LinkedIn messages congratulating me on a 'work anniversary'. The milestone in question was my first year as a Telephone Crisis Support (TCS) worker at Lifeline. As there is evidently a lot of interest and good will towards this extraordinary organization/institution/emergency service and overall force-for-good, I thought I'd share my experience on the frontline.

HOW DID I GET HERE?

My interest in Lifeline began in early 2015. One of the downsides of running my own leadership consultancy business is that it can be isolating at times. I wanted to give back and I was also conscious of the need to interact with groups other than my clients and peers. Lifeline hit the spot. I had a friend who was already a qualified TCS and she said I'd get a lot out of it. Encouraged, I enquired and started the interview and training process.

WORLD-CLASS TRAINING

As an exec mentor and leadership expert, I reckon I am a pretty good judge of training packages. The TCS training I received (run at Lifeline Northern Beaches in Sydney) was excellent. Using a blend of online and classroom learning, the gifted facilitators made sure my intake of 25 trainees was well-equipped to man the phones by graduation time. Make no mistake. This is a serious business. We were being prepared to help people in times of crisis, desolation and despair.

For this reason, the Lifeline TCS training is no tick and flick affair where you just turn up to pass (sadly, all too common in today's 'marketplace' of qualifications). It equips you to understand the issues that callers are likely to have – including mental health, social exclusion, physical health, substance abuse, domestic violence and suicide. It then teaches a proven framework to help people to stay safe until they can access longer-term help. I was particularly impressed by the many role-plays we participated in. It's only through repeatedly rehearsing these deeply personal and often difficult conversations that we are able to help people when they call for real. By the time I was ready to 'fly solo' (under the watchful eye of supervisors), I felt very well prepared.

A DAY IN THE LIFE

I have been 'on the phones' now for 8 months. The picture above is of me on one of my 4 hour evening shifts. I arrive, sign in and, being English, 'grab a cuppa'. Then it's check-in with the supervisor, log on to the call system, put on the headset and click the 'ready' button.

"Hello this is Lifeline, how may we help you?"

ALL THE LONELY PEOPLE

The calls to Lifeline's national crisis number, 13 11 14 are centrally routed, meaning I will be speaking to callers from anywhere in Australia. In my experience so far, many of the calls are from people who are lonely and upset or depressed. Often they are socially isolated. I may be the only person they have spoken to that day. They are usually not suicidal, but that's not to say they are not in crisis or that their call is unwelcome. By simply listening to them for typically 20-40 minutes (though there is no time limit) we are able to help. Most of the time, I find that there is a discernable difference by the end of the call. Callers feel better for sharing their frustrations, fears and feelings – even for just having a moan. The chance to be heard by someone who is trained to be patient, empathetic, and non-judgmental is very soothing. We can't solve their problems – many of which are dire – but we can help them a little. I love it when I get towards the end of the call and the help-seeker's tone is notably lighter. We may even laugh and joke. I'll ask what they plan to do after the call, what they'll eat or what they'll watch on TV. I haven't changed their world, but I may have helped to make it a little brighter, even for a while. Unsurprisingly, many callers are regulars – and that's fine.

THE TOUGH STUFF
Primarily, Lifeline is a suicide support service. The suicide figures in Australia (and most advanced economies) are frightening and getting worse.

In 2014, there were 2,160 males and 704 that died by suicide. This equates to an average of 7.8 deaths by suicide in Australia each day. By comparison, there were 1,200 road deaths.

We are trained to ask every caller – clearly and unambiguously – "are you thinking about killing yourself?" So far, I have helped two people who have replied, "yes" to this question. Tough situations for sure, but I have been able to assist both to stay alive – to 'keep them safe for now'. There are no guarantees of course. We will not always be successful or even know what happens. Crucially, we know we are not responsible for the outcome. All we can do is our best. Based on my two calls, I know I have found it very fulfilling to feel I have been able to help.

SELF-CARE AND SUPPORT

There is usually a team of 4–6 of us on an evening shift at my centre, supported by a supervisor. These are experienced managers who help manage the calls (especially the more complex or suicide-intervention events) and provide feedback. They are also the focus for the self-care support that is at the core of this kind of work. Lifeline is my first exposure to counseling. It is easy to become emotionally affected by the pain and distress we are helping others to navigate. For that reason, there are regular group de-briefing meetings and, after specific incidents (or at any time by request), experts are available to ensure we are OK as we process situations. I certainly feel well-supported in what is a steep learning experience.

JOIN US ON THE BARRICADE?

If you have got this far, chances are you could be the type of person Lifeline needs. In June 2016, over 2,400 Telephone Crisis Support workers manned the phones. This is the frontline for Australians in crisis. I recently heard three separate news pieces in one day on ABC radio referring listeners to call Lifeline on 13 11 14. We took over 1 million calls in 2015 (up over 15% on 2014). This is one place where the pressures of our modern world show up. If, like me, you think things are getting harder for many, expect the caller numbers and the tragic and PREVENTABLE suicide statistics to keep increasing.

It may sound weird, but I really love the work. It has grown me in so many ways and also helps me to be a far better coach and facilitator in my leadership work. You don't have to be particularly empathetic or sensitive. I don't believe that I am either, but the excellent training has equipped me to be effective in resonating with callers so that I am able to help them. I also love that the TCS group is so diverse. There are professionals, students, retirees, psychologists, community service workers, or people, like me, who have no prior experience at all. We are all bound by a common desire to help people going through a rough time. You don't have to be 'on the phones' for very long to realize that could be any one of us.

The pay is terrible, but the reward is priceless!

FIND OUT MORE
If you are interested in finding our more, check out the website:
LIFELINE.ORG.AU/ABOUT-LIFELINE/TRAINING-OPPORTUNITIES

IN CRISIS?
If you, or anyone you know needs crisis support or is contemplating suicide call Lifeline on 13 11 14

Why generosity is good for your bottom line

I recently appeared on Sky Business News to speak about what organisations must do to create a collaborative culture. Whilst we all love the idea of collaboration, it's in short supply. I was reminded of this as I left the Sky studios, walking past a wall of monitors recounting the latest mud-slinging antics of our wannabe leaders Turnbull and Shorten. In the last throes of a too-close-to-call election, collaboration was the last thing on display. And that's a problem. Collaboration is one of the four competencies of the i4 Neuroleader model. As I unpack in a previous post, it consists of the four pillars:

Inspiration
Communication
Generosity
Courage

Generosity is one of the most interesting pillars in the whole model I believe. You see it's a word not typically associated with business, yet one that is so important in helping us to adapt to be both successful and happy in our VUCA world. In the model, Generosity breaks down into 3 elements:

A Win-Win approach
Thinking Beyond Self
Willingness to Help

A Win-Win Approach
This is a big shift. Since our early school days, we've been taught to aspire to individual success. 'Getting ahead' in business has traditionally implied beating colleagues and competitors. We must

re-think this to achieve a more evolved output that draws on collective rather than individual talents and ideas. Forward-thinking classrooms pilots are already exploring ways to do this better, some putting the ability for everyone to write computer code at the centre. As one teacher said in a Four Corners report for the ABC,"I believe that coding is the next layer of literacy and connection."

Thinking Beyond Self
We live in uncertain times. Ironically, it appears to take terrorist acts and natural disasters to bring out the best of us as a species. In extremis, we know to look after each other. We pitch in when storms batter our neighbourhoods and reach out across the globe in the face of suffering and sorrow. The forces that are currently emerging in a poisonous Trump/Clinton US election, Brexit and an insipid Australian election result perhaps mark a time when we question the received wisdom of 'the market', greed and growth. Encouragingly, there are many examples of businesses that are succeeding in part because they wholeheartedly embrace this idea – perhaps through support for community programmes or environmental initiatives.

Willingness to Help
Doing good things for others not only warms the heart, but also protects it. People who regularly volunteer are more likely to use and strengthen their empathetic and altruistic behaviours, as well as improving their own motivation and physical health (through better heart functioning and lower cholesterol levels). I have volunteered for several years now. I serve as a surf lifesaver and, more recently, as a Telephone Crisis Support worker for Lifeline – an organisation in the front line of the fight to reduce the horrific and growing number of suicides in developed economies. I know there is a very tangible reflected benefit and I feel I get back far more than I give.

In a leadership context, taking the time to coach, listen or simply pay undivided attention to those around us can have a surprisingly significant affect. It's easy to miss this simple truth in the rush to 'get stuff done.'

MAKING GENEROSITY HAPPEN

Some simple strategies for developing your own generosity include:

Organise a team-building activity
Cook something for your colleagues or friends
Hand-write a thank you note
Volunteer for a local charity or organisation like Surf Lifesaving or Lifeline
Truly acknowledge the contribution of others

Generosity then is under-regarded, yet highly effective. We all know how wonderful it feels to be on the receiving end of a gift, a thoughtful gesture or a kind word. We see it more often in our home lives than our world of work and I think we are missing a trick. Generosity is good for the sole and, counter-intuitively, the bottom line too.

Give the gift of life

Warning: This week's Pinch of Thought discusses the issue of suicide. Some readers, for any number of reasons, may wish to skip this.

On Monday December 14th, 80 men gathered to remember a mate. We've come together across many years and many walks, united by our love for rugby – a game that we all play (some well, some not so). We are the Newport Nasties, a band of brothers, doing life together. The fact that so many came at such short notice at a crazy-busy time of year is testament to how much our mate was loved and valued. Yet – just 48 hours before – he felt so friendless, isolated and utterly hopeless that he took his own life. His family, friends and our wider community are confused, angry, speechless, bereft and ultimately very, very sad.

'TIS THE SEASON
Tragically, we will not be the only ones. This model created by the charity Beyond Blue maps the factors that can combine to create the conditions in which suicide seems like the best, or least-worst choice. It's easy to forget, yet obvious if we pause to think, that many of these factors are heightened at this time of year. Christmas for many is hellish. Broken relationships are amplified, loneliness is heightened and, of course, our love affair with booze and drugs simply lubricates the process.

Suicide Warning Signs

- FEELING WORTHLESS
- FEELING TRAPPED
- A sense of HOPELESSNESS OR NO HOPE for the FUTURE
- SOCIAL ISOLATION or FEELING ALONE
- ALCOHOL and DRUG misuse
- AGGRESSIVENESS and IRRITABILITY
- GIVING things AWAY
- Possessing LETHAL MEANS
- Feeling like you DON'T BELONG
- FEELING LIKE A BURDEN to others
- ENGAGING in "risky" BEHAVIORS
- A HISTORY of SUICIDAL BEHAVIOUR
- FREQUENTLY TALKING about DEATH
- DRAMATIC changes in MOOD and BEHAVIOUR

beyondblue
Depression. Anxiety

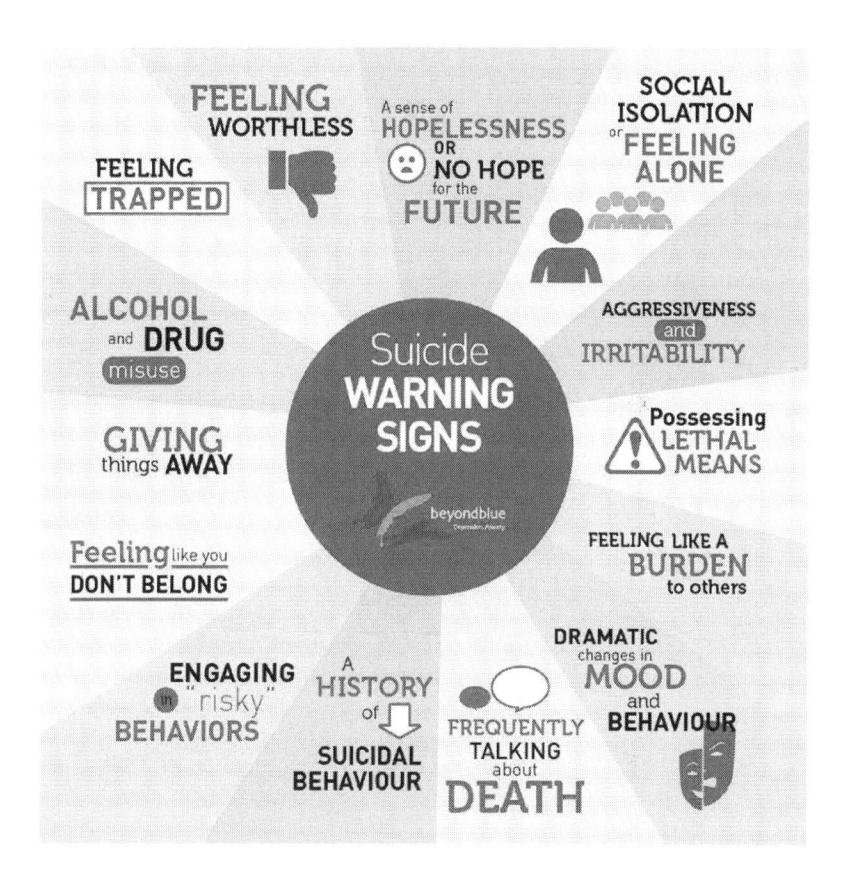

CHILLING FIGURES

You may be familiar with these Australian figures, but they are no less stark for that. The UK is no different.

Suicide remains the leading cause of death for Australians aged 15 to 44. In 2012, 1,901 males (16.8 per 100,000) and 634 females (5.6 per 100,000) died by suicide.

- Deaths by suicide have reached a 10-year peak.
- Men account for three out of every five deaths by suicide
- The most recent ABS data shows that almost twice as many

people died from suicide in Australia, than in road related transport deaths (1,310 vs 2,535)
- For every completed suicide, it is estimated that as many as 30 people attempt.
- It is estimated that around 1,000 people think about suicide every day.

LET'S TACKLE THIS BY TALKING

There are many bad things in the world that we can't change. Reducing suicide is not one of them. It is doable and we can all help. We need to bring it into the open. Our mate's death did that and many of us shared stories. Several told – for the first time – how they had contemplated ending their life. Ironically, perversely and painfully, these were and are good conversations for us to be having. As we slip into the festive season, let's be mindful of how others are REALLY doing. HAVE THIS CONVERSATION. With a bit of down time, there's no better time to talk with your family and friends. If in doubt, ask them the question – are you feeling suicidal? Encourage them to seek help – **Lifeline 131114** and **Beyond Blue 1300 22 4636 (AU)** and **Samaritans 116123 (UK)** offer support 24/7. There is an army of great people ready to help. They come from a place of love. You will probably never know, but your actions may just give someone the gift of life. That's got to be better than an iPhone6S.

Why it pays to give

I love that Mark Zuckerburg has declared he'll be gifting 99% of the value of his shares in little ol' Facebook for charitable purposes. That's 99% of $US45 billion. True, it still leaves Mr and Mrs Z a lazy $US450 million (if I've got my zeros right) to squeeze by on, but it's still pretty cool. Inspired by Bill Gates, it's setting a great challenge that many other well-healed Americans are keen to take up. Pioneered by Gates and Warren Buffet, the idea is for the super-wealthy to sign up for 'The Giving Pledge'. The plan? To give away half of their wealth over their lifetimes. Sadly, the super-rich in Australia present fewer shining examples. Nothing is more pathetic than the ongoing soap of our richest mineral magnate family fighting over their share of $11 billion like seagulls around a few dropped chips. Or a certain Mr Rupert Murdoch who, when approached by philanthropist Dick Smith to get on board the giving love train said, "I don't believe in foundations."

WHAT CAN WE DO?
The good news is most of us do much better. We may not be building hospital wings or wind farms, but every little helps. On the philanthropic medal table, Australia sits 5th, but will take comfort from pushing the stingy Poms into 6th place! The Germans are 20th and the French a less-than-magnifique 74th.

VOLUNTEERING ROCKS
Where I personally love to contribute is as a volunteer (where Australians are surely the gold medalists!) I know my two favourite experiences this year have been volunteer-based.

LIFELINE 1

I've grown immensely through my training to man the suicide crisis line as a Lifeline (131144) call support worker. I know I get far more than I give. The sense of satisfaction that comes from bringing even a small sense of hope or relief to someone in a really dark, lonely place is extraordinary.

LIFELINE 2

My other lifeline is more literal. I volunteer as a surf lifesaver. Every Sunday, I join the Water Safety team at Nippers (a beach club for kids aged 6–15). My job is to help the less confident nippers to swim out to a buoy 150 metres off the beach. That can be very daunting. I love helping the kids to do so much more than they think they can. Tears turn to smiles. Confidence grows. Priceless. These are obviously personal things, but I think the benefits of giving are universal. It's good for us as an individual, good for us as a community and good for us as part of an organization. If you have not tried it, it's time you did. There is a wonderful glow that comes from being part of something that is greater than just us. It's also a brilliant way to build personal leadership and bring teams together, so looking for opportunities to give as a team is both intrinsically good and business smart. Clever leaders get this – even if we are leading just 'team me'! We may not be able to quite flash the cash like the Zuckerburgs, but that's no reason we can't get the same sense of satisfaction from putting others first.

WANTED: First-rate intelligence

I've always been fond of English literature. I studied it as one of the three A Levels (the UK equivalent of HSC) and, 35 years on, I still remember loving one of the set authors, the American F Scott Fitzgerald. Fitzgerald is best known for his works, 'The Great Gatsby' and 'Tender is the Night'. Like any good lit student, I could rattle off quote after quote, like *"Her voice is full of money"*, or *"So you ruined me, did you? ...Then we're both ruined..."*. The deeper side of this troubled soul was explored in a collection titled 'The Crack Up'. Its most famous quote is his observation that.

> *The test of a first-rate intelligence is the ability to hold two opposed ideas in the mind at the same time, and still retain the ability to function.*

I am not sure that I understood its meaning as a young man, but, it now speaks to me as a keen observation as to what is lacking in so many of our leaders.

DUMBING IT DOWN
I write this just a few days after Brexit and in the last death throws of an Australian election campaign, that has been as uninspiring as it was long. Without getting into the morass of either, there is a uniting theme; 'leaders' of all persuasions portraying a world of simple choices. "In or out?" "Tax or spend?" "Growth or fairness?"

THE TRUTH IS INCONVENIENTLY UNTIDY
Our world is far less binary. As leaders, we have to navigate our businesses and people through uncharted waters in the face of accelerating change and continuous disruption. 'Last-year-plus-a-bit thinking' no longer cuts it. We have to innovate, to trust our gut,

to guess, to make-it-up. We must be prepared to fail and treat that failure as a positive step. Against this reality the 'cast-iron' proclamations of Shorten/Turnbull as to where the budget will be in 10 years, (when they can't tell you where the iron ore price will sit next Tuesday) are literally incredible.

HOLDING THE TENSION

Pollies simplify everything because they believe they must to get message 'cut through'. To an extent, it's true that complex thinking and messaging can get lost (or twisted) in translation. Sadly, it may also be true that this childlike parroting or mantras like "jobs and growth" *is* effective in the confines of an 8-week election campaign.

It's a harder game for our business leaders. Dumbing it down does not work across 52 weeks. To succeed in the face of a VUCA world of Vulnerability, Uncertainty, Complexity and Ambiguity, we surely need Fitzgerald's 'first-rate intelligence'. We need leaders who can hold in a positive tension apparently contradictory forces; for example the need to improve productivity with fewer staff whilst simultaneously improving the level of people care.

SIMPLEXITY IS KEY

Rather than dumb it down, we must smarten it down. Think of the effort that smart phone designers put into creating one digit, intuitive 'buttons' that sit on top of literally thousands of options and permutations. In the same way, our leadership needs to be both simple to understand and access, yet nuanced and bespoke in the way it is felt by an individual. This is Simplexity – the complex made simple (accessible and elegant). It puts a premium on ideas, collaboration and innovation. As About My Brain Institute founder Silvia Damiano says, it is why we are now in the Imagination Age – an age that demands so much more from its leaders than to simply be experienced or intelligent

UP FOR THE CHALLENGE?

As leaders then we need to step up. We need to think at a higher level and we need to think twice. Firstly about the solutions to the new challenges we face. Secondly about the best way to connect those ideas to move, inform and inspire those we lead. For a generation or more, many leaders have been asleep at the wheel – able to succeed simply by repeating cookie cutter solutions. As is now clear, that time is past. We need the 'first-rate intelligences' as defined by Fitzgerald a century ago.

Are you up for that challenge?

Preparing ourselves for high performance in testing times

Performance is probably the most common word in the business lexicon. We have *performance indicators, performance management, business performance, personal performance* and of course *high performance*. Performance is at the heart of what we strive to achieve as leaders – for ourselves our teams and our organisations.

Delivering consistent levels of high performance has never been easy, but in today's VUCA world, it's harder than ever. It is one thing to perform well on one project or perhaps to turn in a good set of numbers over a quarter or half. It's quite another to perform at a consistently high level year after year in the face of our increasingly volatile and stressed business environments.

TIME FOR TENNIS?
We can gain a useful insight as to how we may need to adapt from the sports arena. If we look to the world of tennis there are four men who stand head and shoulders above the rest in terms of consistent performance. There are any number of young tyros with extraordinary skill who can win a magic set and even a match or two. But the Grand Slam finals, encounters that can last for 4 or 5 hours, are invariably contested by just four men – Novak Djokovic, Andy Murray, Roger Federer and Rafa Nadal. Over the best-of-five set matches, these are they guys who can perform time and again. On top of their incredible natural talent, they have layered great discipline and thorough physical and mental conditioning. They understand the importance of diet, sleep, rest and complete mental preparation. Additionally, they have to take total personal responsibility. Whilst supported by a team of experts – physios, coaches, sports psychologists and dieticians, it is the players alone

who must perform completely unassisted during a match. This intensive and holistic preparation' is what enables them to perform both athletically and psychologically whilst under the most intense physical and emotional pressure.

EQUIPPING OURSELVES TO PERFORM

As business leaders we need to follow their lead. We must prepare ourselves for sustained high performance. We are all being asked to do more with less against a backdrop of continual change. Our lives are now a blur of stress and mental health issues are showing up both at work and home with damaging consequences for our families and colleagues. So what do we need to do to perform consistently well?

Performance is one of the 4 key Competencies in the i4 Neuroleader model developed by Silvia Damiano, founder of the About My Brain Institute. (The others are *Collaboration, Innovation* and *Agility*). We define Performance as follows:

Performance refers to the optimal level, both mental and physical, that a person is able to achieve when implementing a task.

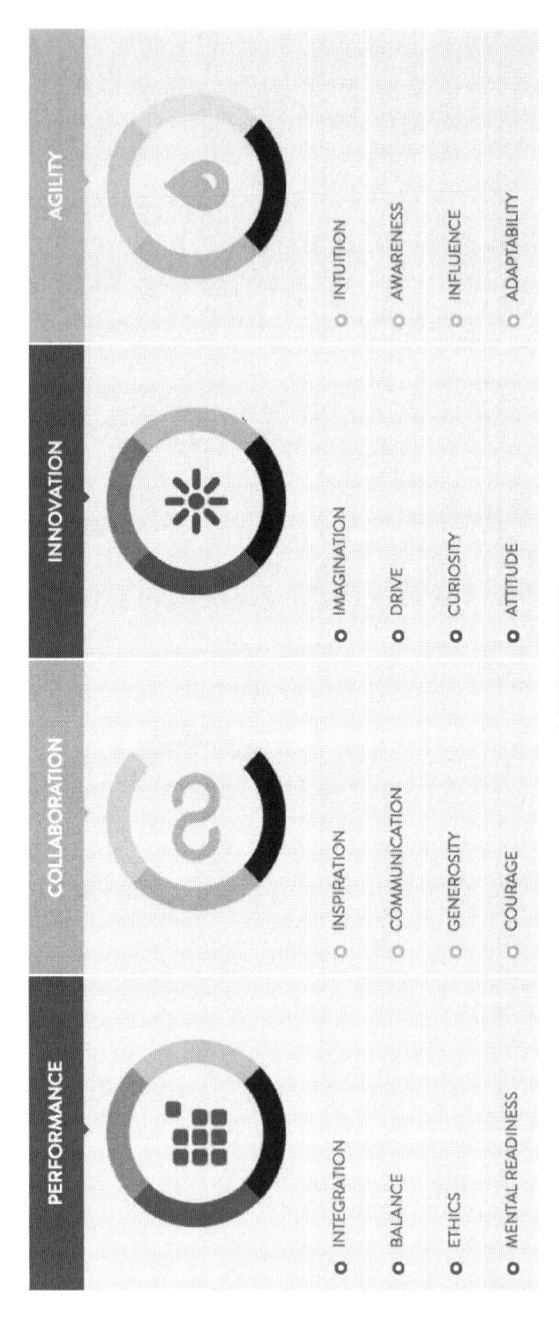

PERFORMANCE	COLLABORATION	INNOVATION	AGILITY
○ INTEGRATION	○ INSPIRATION	○ IMAGINATION	○ INTUITION
○ BALANCE	○ COMMUNICATION	○ DRIVE	○ AWARENESS
○ ETHICS	○ GENEROSITY	○ CURIOSITY	○ INFLUENCE
○ MENTAL READINESS	○ COURAGE	○ ATTITUDE	○ ADAPTABILITY

© SILVIA DAMIANO

To really understand performance then, we need to look at the integration of both our mental and physical states and think about what a task is, not just in terms of time, but what it requires from our brain.

THE FOUR PILLARS OF PERFORMANCE

The Competency of Performance breaks down further into four parts or Pillars; integration, balance, ethics and mental readiness.

1. *Integration*

   This is about effectively bringing together various parts of our brain and body to create a balanced system. When we do this well, we are likely to be calm, but alert, mindful, energised and easy to work with.

   Key elements are:

   Executive function
   Mind-Body alignment and
   The 'Care' factor

   Executive Function is all about getting the best from the Pre-Frontal Cortex area of our brain. It's involved in decision-making, planning, abstract reasoning and judgment. The first stage in Mind-Body alignment is for leaders to be able to perceive their emotions and then align their three brains (head, heart and gut) to govern their actions and decisions. This enables us to perform better and more consistently – irrespective of external stressors. It also enables us to be mindful of better splitting our attention between task and people care – a failure point for most 'busy' leaders.

2. *Balance*
   The brain's balanced state is better managed when we assign time and attention to actions that can assist us to deal with stress and adversity without affecting our performance. Key factors are:

   Physicality
   Down time and
   Sociability

   Physicality is about eating well, exercising and allocating time for relaxation and play. We know this to be important, but so often ignore this need – often like a badge of honour. When work train at the gym, the actual strengthening of muscles takes place in the rest days afterwards – when the muscles repair in response to the stress. In the same way, creating time to re-charge, relax, to socialise with others and to think is not just a nice-to-do, but a vital part of the process in building performance and resilience.

3. *Ethics*
   Ethics is the act of reflecting and finding congruence among our, emotions, thoughts and actions. Core elements are:

   Values
   Judgment and
   Congruency

   We must be clear on our values – and aware of how they will inform our thinking – and use our judgment to understand, evaluate and make considered decisions. In a business world where the moral compass can appear hopelessly debased, getting clear on what we stand for is vital for both ourselves and our teams. Finally we must be congruent. This implies saying what we mean and demonstrating it in every sense (body language, tone, attitude, facial expression and actions).

4. *Mental Readiness*
This refers to our ability to create a balanced psychological state in which we can perform at an optimal level. It's about:

Confidence
Focus and
Planning

Firstly, we need create a state of internal confidence to act. We must be able to plan ahead, using skills such as visualisation and physically prepared (by centering and breathing). Crucially, we must develop our ability to focus and refocus. A person who is mentally ready has mastered the capacity to focus, self-manage and maintain a healthy degree of internal discipline.

WHEN WE DO THIS BADLY
Responding to the increased work/life pressure by simply working harder in our long-established and unquestioned work rituals, leads to a steady decline in our performance. At an individual level, we can lack self-awareness, lose control of our emotions and become inconsistent between what we say and do. This feeds into poor business performance with a likelihood of increased conflict, poor strategy and planning, unethical choices and heightened levels of stress, absenteeism and even mental illness. This is neither a happy nor productive workplace!

WHEN WE DO THIS WELL
When we reframe the performance equation to include the brain, things can look very different. By taking care of our mind, body

and spirit, we can be confident without being arrogant and remain calm in stressful situations. We can rely on our good judgment and be focused, disciplined and know how to prioritise. This is good for business. We are more productive and efficient. We contribute to more resourceful and solution-driven teams and make better decisions. We end up with a brain-friendly culture that is both a better place to work and be, but is also likely to have much higher levels of performance (and reduced levels of absenteeism, disengagement, turnover and mental illness).

When we break it down, so much of this is common sense. It is something we know to be innately true. We *know* that we are at our best when we are rested, balanced and calm. We *know* that acting on our instinctive empathy builds connection and contributes to a great culture. We *know* that good planning, discipline and consciously working on getting the best out of ourselves and others is the way to great performance. But in the pressure cooker of business as usual we seem to so easily lose track, to wing it, or perform only sporadically.

If we are going emulate the great tennis players to win our own Grand Slams, we need to take a leaf from their book and adopt an ongoing whole-of-body and-mind approach.

It pays to walk!

FITBIT FANBOYS
There's no little irony that it has taken a technological gizmo to provoke business leaders across Australia to get off their corporate bums and engage in that lowest tech of activities – the humble walk. If you've not heard, the Fitbit is a watch-like device that measures the number of steps taken by its wearer each day. IT research group Gartner estimates over 65 million electronic fitness devices like the Fitbit will be sold in 2015. The phenomenon is infecting workplaces, with co-workers competing to win the stepping war. There are some interesting behavioural principles behind the trend.

IT'S MEASURABLE
Like most business gadgets, the Fitbit is destined for landfill. For now though, it provides a simple metric of activity and reaffirms the old mantra that "what gets measured gets done".

IT'S TARGETABLE
Wearers set a daily step target, encouraging them to change their behaviour. That may mean taking the stairs rather than the lift, or treating the dog to an evening stroll to hit the daily number.

IT'S PLAYFUL
Whilst some uber execs doubtless see their step-count as yet another way to demonstrate their superiority, for most workers, it's the playful nature of comparing results that encourages them to stay in the step game. There's a clear sense of progression – one of our key human motivators – and we know it's also good for us.

MEETINGS GET RE-BOOTED
Perhaps the biggest benefit of the Fitbit craze though is the way it

is encouraging some leaders to re-evaluate the way they operate. Meetings do nothing for the step-count, meaning there is more incentive to keep them short. Even better, meetings on the run are happening. The walk 'n talks that used to occur only in TV dramas (remember the West Wing), with 3 or 4 people walking purposefully around the building resolving geo-politics, sales strategy or the footy comp are now taking place in the real world as step-hungry execs seek to keep the step count ticking over. Likewise, phone calls are now made on the hoof. In a recent Australian Financial Review article, Rio Tinto MD and Fitbit convert, Andrew Harding shared his new habit of walking around his office precinct rather than sitting whilst on the phone. "It's good for stress management and it motivates me to be healthy".

WALKING'S GOOD FOR CULTURE TOO
Some businesses are running Fitbit competitions across disciplines and even between different locations. As a result, they are seeing new connections and conversations taking place. Step-count it appears is the universal language crossing all boundaries! I recently ran a Leading Change masterclass and met Bill, a senior technical leader in a large power distribution company. We spent a lot of time talking about the challenges facing the business. One of these was the gap between the predominantly older and male engineering departments and the younger IT team. Bill shared that he is a keen walker. He started walking ten years ago to lose weight, and grew to love the benefits. He also treks in the local mountains at the weekends. He mentioned this to some of the IT guys and 3 of them asked to come along. They had a great time and were also able to start to brainstorm some ways they could work together. News got out and Bill has a list of 15 or so lined up for his next trek. It's a lovely example of how inter-generational barriers CAN be breached in often surprising ways.

WALKING THE TALK?
If Fitbit has not taken off in your world, maybe it's time to give it a go. I love that anyone in your business can introduce the idea. It's accessible to everyone, breaks down barriers, encourages us to challenge outdated business paradigms (like long meetings) and is good for our heart and our sole!!!

▰ Are you sitting uncomfortably?

There's a lovely image in *The Simpsons* that shows how Homer's favourite couch is so well-used that it has become sculpted to fit the shape of his ample rear like a glove. Reclined in front of the TV, remote in one hand and a cold Duff beer in the other, our cartoon anti-hero is a wonderful comic observation of pretty much everything we need to avoid as aspiring thought leaders. Whether we like it or not, we are stuck in the fast lane to change and it's never going to stop!

THAT'S A BIG STATEMENT
Traditional change management strategies are typically presented as the process of transitioning a business from one state (broken) through a change intervention to a new stable state (fixed). In other words, it assumes that change is a relatively temporary state that we need to negotiate (or endure) before arriving at a new stable stage. Problem is, that's not how it is. Change is now continuous and, to become and remain successful as business people and influencers, we need to continuously adapt.

THE LUXURY OF CERTAINTY IS DEAD
As human beings, we crave security and comfort. Left alone, many of us would love to take a seat alongside Homer on the couch. Learning how to be comfortable within a state of continuous disturbance demands some shifts in our mindset and approach. Here are five that I've found that help me.

1. *Let go of perfectionism*
   It's a luxury we can't afford and one that rarely serve us. The pareto principle is a great rule of thumb. 80% good, done quickly is enough to test our ideas and products. It's about getting your

idea, project or product to a minimum viable stage – i.e. good enough to test in the market. If it's good and gains traction, you can polish, refine and perfect later.

2. *Celebrate former achievements… then move on.*
We can tend to over-rely on and over-value past achievements and thinking. This prevents us from adopting the teachable mindset that we all need move forward. Make no mistake, we're living through a change revolution. Business models that have been successful for decades are now being disrupted and rendered irrelevant in months. The thinking and actions that made us successful in the past are by no means guaranteed to propel us to future success. So raise a glass to your past successes… then consign them to history so you can look forward with an open mind.

3. *Change your environment*
Prospering in uncertainty requires us to be nimble, flexible and open. We need to challenge and break habits that lock us into old patterns. Shaking up our working environment is a great way to do this. So move around, de-clutter, explore different spaces (libraries and cafes are great) and mobile technologies that will help inspire you.

4. *Be like Madonna*
In the same vein, you may want to re-think what you wear. We can all benefit from a bit of 'material girl' re-invention. This may be dressing more casually, more formally or actively developing a personal brand 'look'. All have their place (I'm moving back to suits as I they make me feel more confident and match with my positioning).

5. ***Lighten up***

    It's a rollercoaster journey we're on. With so much ambiguity, so many unknowns, we are going to be wrong, we are going to fail and we are going to stuff up. None of us can be certain what will succeed 's but we ARE having a go. One of the great things about continuous change is that all of our failures will rapidly be consigned to history. So learning to laugh at ourself is a good idea (I do this a lot – encouraged by my family who are already doing it for me).

I hope some of these help. In the event you are looking for further inspiration you may want to ignore these three pearls of wisdom from our couch potato mentor, Homer.

> *Trying is the first step towards failure.*

> *You don't like your job? You don't strike. You go in every day and do it really half-assed. That's the American way.*

and

> *If something is to hard to do, then it's not worth doing.*

The power of doing nothing

I recently returned from the World Masters Games in New Zealand. We came up empty in the hunt for surfboat rowing medal glory. Team 'Crusty' scored a creditable fifth, but sadly those Kiwis don't play at sport! Hardened crews the lot of 'em. No out-of-condition pub crews, or last-minute ring-ins attempting to recapture long-past glory days. Bugger!

Already I am missing the regular training. Not so much from the physical angle (there are other ways to stay fit) but from a mental perspective. You see, the great thing about rowing is that it's not only good for the body, it also clears the mind. Out in the ocean, connected with nature and concentrating on big things (like not getting smashed) or small things (like a technical improvement), it's impossible to think about anything else. The brain gets a break and it's much-needed.

"MY BRAIN NEEDS A HOLIDAY"
I was reminded of this in a recent conversation. My client has been pushing very hard for a long time trying to work out what the next chapter of her life will look like. Supremely capable, smart and driven, she's finally realized that the answer needs time to form. For her, it's time to pull back, not press on. As she reflected so wonderfully, "my brain needs a holiday".

SOMETIMES WE JUST NEED TO STOP
Many of us are losing the art of the pause. In our headlong rush for instant information, instant results and instant gratification, the default is to always push on. We work longer, squeeze more in and juggle work/life commitments – badly. It can look like progress, but often feels like anything but. In my executive coaching work,

this is a common finding. It shows up as an absence of balance. Physical health, mental health, family time and nutrition are all out of whack. The result is often stressed, absent, unhappy, unfit and – ironically – poor-performing leaders.

GET FIT WATCHING TV
When we are at the gym pumping iron or busily going nowhere on our spin cycles, we're not actually building our muscles, we're tearing them. The muscle-strengthening process happens as the tears are repaired – when we are resting. If we don't rest, the muscle builds more slowly. The excess effort is a waste of time and energy. We are just spinning our wheels.

In the same way, taking the time to pause, rest and reflect is an essential part of training our brains. When we do this well we develop clarity, regain perspective and ultimately make better decisions. In our 'go-hard-or-go-home' world that can be easy to forget.

SO WHAT ARE YOU NOT GOING TO DO?
On my bedside table, I have a pile of unread business books by some amazing authors. I get a couple of chapters in and then get distracted as another 'hot' title arrives. Truth is, by the time I get to bed I am pooped. My brain is full. It's not the right time to be topping up with the latest from Seth Godin, Elizabeth Gilbert or Malcolm Gladwell.

Whilst there are hacks through book summary services like Blinkist, that misses the point. The process of reading a book – slowly and luxuriously is relaxing, like a good massage or a walk in the mountains. My father recently told me that he was reading the whole of the Game of Thrones series. That's 3,500 pages of blood, sex, death, ambition and dragons. It's also a journey of escapism and brain-fuel – far removed from the day-to-day business of life (for most of us!). I think I might just join Dad on the journey as a way to rest and refuel.

There are many other things you can stop doing to create the time and space for your body and mind to relax, of course. Saying no to invitations, reducing travel and taking up immersive activities (like rowing) all help. It's about building the discipline to do less, not more.

Try it. You may be pleasantly surprised by how much you can get done!

Why connection trumps capability

I recently ran a leadership workshop where I showed Dr Brené Brown's excellent Ted talk. I've watched it many times and usually concentrate on the section where she discusses vulnerability. But this time I was struck by Brené's first point – about the reason we exist.

> *Connection is why we're here. It's what gives purpose and meaning to our lives.*

That's pretty profound! It's also a long way from where many of us find ourselves. Whilst technology enables us to 'connect' as never before, the irony is that many of us have never felt more isolated.

I thought of this again in two recent client interactions. The first was when I facilitated an event for a technical company in the process of developing its thought leadership. The business knows that to succeed it must move away from the historical low-margin conversations around products and specifications. It's now building new positioning as a future-focused influencer – far more attuned to customer needs and aspirations.

The second was a conversation with an executive in a financial planning business. They are struggling to adapt in the face of new 'DIY' financial software and low-cost, outsourced solutions that are slashing margins. Their traditional model of impersonal, infrequent and expensive customer interactions is busted.

CONNECTION TRUMPS CAPABILITY

Both cases illustrate an opportunity that many miss. In a rush to trumpet our credentials and technical know-how we fail to first connect. In a world of same-same offerings, connection, not capability is the edge we need.

TALK LIKE A REAL PERSON!
I am lucky enough to work closely with several neuroscientists through the About My Brain Institute. In truth, most of them roll their eyes when I talk about left-brain and right-brain. It's simplistic to say all of our emotions and feelings reside in the right hemisphere of the brain. Simplistic, but useful. Whatever the truth of the (grey) matter, we're heavily influenced by our feelings and our emotions – not just by our logical (left) brain. Yet most businesses make a poor fist of creating an emotional connection. They fail to make the right-brain case to support their rational, data-driven argument.

GETTING STARTED
Doing this is actually not that hard. We do it all the time in our non-business conversations. The biggest barrier is our own prejudice about exactly what 'business' should look and sound like.

We've been schooled in the formal, the fact-based, the logical and the linear. All good stuff – and still essential. Where the gap (and opportunity) lies is in also connecting at a human level.

So tell great stories. Ask questions. Enquire about what's going on in your client's personal world. Make them feel heard. Display your own fears and vulnerabilities. Tell a joke. Empathise.

Inspire them. Excite them. Share their risk. Challenge them to step up, be brave, go first, run a pilot, make a difference, live a little, dare to fail.

When we do this, we are more likely to genuinely connect. Our relationship evolves from transactional (seller-buyer) to collaborative (partnering) to solve a problem or maybe create something exciting, special or unique.

SOFT SKILLS – HARD CASH

And don't be fooled, there's money in them 'connection' hills. A large Australian insurer has recently embarked on a complete overhaul of the way it manages workers returning to the workforce after sickness. It has moved from a linear process (this-is-where-you-should-be-by-10 weeks/14 weeks/18 weeks) to a case-management approach. Now, specially trained staff are heavily involved with the care and recuperation of the insurees. They are encouraged to build a caring and supportive relationship. Not only does this make for great customer service, the stats show that, on average, workers are returning to their roles 20-30% sooner (and therefore no longer claiming on the insurance). The shift to an ostensibly 'softer', approach with high levels of human connection is making plenty of hard cash.

Whatever business you are in, there are likely to be similar upsides from creating a more human connection with customers, staff and suppliers.

So soften the **** up!

What price success?

I wrote recently about the power of connection. In an ironic twist, today my internet connection died – predictably at a supremely inconvenient moment. This created a farcical 'signal quest' as I frantically ran like an addict from café to café, *"do you have wi-fi, do you have wi-fi?"* Finally somewhere did. Message sent. Mission accomplished. Celebratory cappuccino consumed! But still I found myself mentally exhausted.

As a solopreneur, the load can be heavy. I returned to my home office and spoke to the Head of IT. That would be me! I'm also head of Finance, Marketing, Strategy, Sales, Delivery, Research, Operations, Fleet, Stationery and Pets. That's a lot for one person.

EXECUTIVE OVERWHELM IS EVERYWHERE
This overwhelm is not confined solely to the solos. Increasingly, I find my executive mentoring clients are looking for help to balance their professional and private lives. They find themselves trapped in a world of busyness. At work they can become stressed and unproductive. They stay back late to catch up. Once home, tired and distracted, they're not really present. Relationships suffer, stress increases and the cycle is reinforced. Fallout in terms of marriage breakdown, job loss, mental health issues and addictions are all increasing.

I don't have a flip solution to this. I do believe many of us have got things out of whack.

The drivers are many. We want to contribute, to succeed, to provide. We love to learn and grow, to create teams, projects, products and businesses that we can be proud of. Less attractively, ambition, fear, ego and greed can all contribute.

In the pressure cooker of the modern world, perhaps we've simply stopped making the time to listen and think. Consequently, we've lost site of what's really important.

THINKING TIME
What we can do is to pause and reflect. Some questions I find helpful are:

Am I happy?
Am I living the life I want?
Am I spending time with the people who matter to me?
What does success look like for me and am I achieving it?
Am I making the difference I was born to make?
What can I stop doing to create more time?

FOLLOW YOUR HEART
I don't believe that any of this means we have to give up our ambitions or our big jobs. But we do need to think carefully about who and what's really important and allocate our time, care and attention accordingly.

When we follow our hearts, the answers are pretty clear. We just need to get out of our own way to make sure we are not winning in one area only to find we've lost where it really counts.

Time to get empathy into your leadership mix?

I'm currently doing a lot of exec mentoring work. What's striking are the high levels of stress and stretch I see in so many of my mentees. Corporate is a tough place right now. There's a relentless pressure to 'perform' – to do more with less, and faster. Many execs are routinely working 50, 60 and even 70 hour weeks in their attempt to keep up and 'deliver'.

In this pressure cooker of expectation, it's unsurprising that many of the 'soft' skills are overlooked. The key one is empathy. I find that many men in particular (though not exclusively) struggle to be empathetic. 'Soft stuff' doesn't come easily. The overriding "get shit done' business imperative absolves them from the need to challenge this. But they are missing out. Empathy is not only good for the soul, it's key to leading both ourselves and others.

EMPATHY-BY-NUMBERS

I think we convince ourselves that we either 'are', or 'are not' empathetic. That's a cop out. We're all capable of empathy – some of us just have to work at it. I know because I'm one of them. My wife, a counselor, is wonderfully empathetic. It's innate in her. She *'feels'* others needs first and *'thinks'* second.

For me, it's a recently-learned process. I man the phones for Lifeline, the leading response agency for Australians in crisis. As part of their excellent training, I was taught to be empathetic-by-numbers. This involves responding to a caller's situation by acknowledging first how they must be feeling. So rather than rush to judge or solve a callers situation (my typical rational responses), I'll recognize and respond to the emotion that sits behind it. I say things like:

"That must be so distressing for you"

or

"Wow, it sounds as if you've had a tough day, would you like us to talk about that?"

In truth, it sometimes feels forced (though never false). But here's the thing – IT WORKS! The act of empathizing, however clumsy it may feel, never fails to illicit a response. In this sense, I *'think'* first and then *'feel'* the emotional response second. It's like an echo that immediately forms a powerful, intimate and personal connection. As Pakistani writer Mohsin Hamid puts it,

> *Empathy is about finding echoes of another person in yourself.*

EMPATHY AS A LEADERSHIP TOOL

In leadership jargon, we often talk about engagement, collaboration and motivation. Developing our empathy is a fantastic way to build the emotional connections that underpin all of these. To do so, we must make the time to genuinely enquire about how our team members and the people and events that are important to them are going. Oh and we need to listen too! This is both good for us and the bottom-line. As Stephen Covey wrote:

> *When you show deep empathy toward others, their defensive energy goes down and positive energy replaces it. That's when you can get more creative in solving problems.*

GIVE IT A CRACK

As I wrote in 'The Power of Doing Nothing', it's easy to fall into the trap of ever-increasing busyness as a response to increasing our productivity. Authentically engaging with those around you by creating the time and headspace to genuinely connect is undoubtedly a smarter and more pleasurable approach.

If empathy doesn't come easily, I'd really encourage you to experiment along the lines I suggest. Your staff will appreciate the effort, even if it initially feels a bit mechanical. I'm finding it gets easier, is personally rewarding and undoubtedly helps me to get the best out of those I work with.

That's got to be worth a try right?

Printed in Great Britain
by Amazon